Down on the Farm:
Red Clay & Rocks, Faith & Hope

"A Have to Is a Hard Way to Go!"

Stories, Pictures, and Tales
of the McCain Family of Waxhaw, North Carolina
and Including the Walkup, Pickens, and Winslow
Connections

Compiled and Recorded by
Gladys Elizabeth McCain Kerr

Createspace: The Amazon Group
Charleston, South Carolina
2015

An Old Irish Blessing
willi
May love and laughter light your days,
and warm your heart and home.
May good and faithful friends be yours,
wherever you may roam.
May peace and plenty bless your world
with joy that long endures.
May all life's passing seasons bring the best to you and yours!

Acknowledgements

With grateful appreciation to my cousins who provided stories, pictures, support, and encouragement: Jo Nell and Bob McCain, Lynn McCain Twitty, Harry Lake McCain, Rosemary McCain, Karen McCain Baxley, Betty and Joe Ewart McCain, Albert and Hazel Starnes, Phonzo and Clara Starnes, Franklin Norwood, Phyllis Simpson Garner, Lynn Rogers Stikeleather, Diane Countryman, Ernie and Elaine Creech, Kathy Stubbs, Ann Sappenfield, Mary Bass, Rhonda Brady McManus, and Rachel Gordon Brady. My brother Robert and his wife Drake were also most helpful with information about my immediate family.

This book is a tribute to my parents, Robert Maxwell McCain, Sr., and Isa Gladys Winslow McCain, and to my grandfather, Robert Thompson McCain (April 24, 1860-June 11, 1927) and my grandmother, Mary Elizabeth Walkup McCain (February 22, 1868-March 24, 1953)

A special note of appreciation to Maurice Thomas for his additional research and preparation of photos and the final manuscript for publication.

ISBN: 13: 978-1514163979
ISBN: 10: 1514163977

Dedicated to

my grandson Williams McCain Kerr
and
my son James Maxwell Kerr

James and McCain,
I want you to know your grandmothers and grandfathers,
your aunts and uncles, and your cousins.

CONTENTS

"A Have To Is a Hard Way to Go"

McCain, Who Are You? Before I begin stories of my McCain grandparents, I would like to give first a brief background of the Walkup and Pickens lineage and then show how they are related to the McCains. These families were Scots-Irish Presbyterians who along with the Jacksons, McCamies, McWhorters, McCammans, Crawfords, Osbornes, and others settled on Waxhaw Creek around 1751, and they were loyal to the American Colonists in their struggle for independence. Your great-great-grandmother Mary Elizabeth Walkup McCain was a descendant of Captain James Alexander Walkup (born 1724 in Ireland), the first of the Walkups (Wachoups) in America, and his wife Margaret Nancy Pickens. Capt. Walkup died in Old Lancaster, South Carolina, in 1789. He married Margaret Pickens, the daughter of Israel Sidney Pickens (born 1693 Antrim, Ireland-died 1749 in Virginia) who came to America with his parents and other siblings including Andrew Samuel Pickens in 1722. The Province of Antrim is on the northeast coast of what is today Northern Ireland. These Scots-Irish families had left Scotland in the 1600's and settled in Ulster (Northern Ireland). In the early 1700's many of these families left Ireland for America to escape discrimination and religious persecution. Often entire congregations left for the New World, settling first in Pennsylvania then later following the Great Wagon Road through Virginia to the Carolina frontier where they settled on land abandoned by the Waxhaw Indians who had been descimated by the small pox epidemic of 1741.

Your family also includes the Revolutionary War soldier Maj. Gen. Andrew Pickens, born in Paxton, Bucks County, Pennsylvania, September 13, 1739. His father and your ancestor Israel Sidney Pickens were brothers who came to America in 1722. Like many other Scots-Irish families, the family of the future revolutionary soldier Andrew Pickens moved from Pennsylvania to Virginia and ultimately joined the Waxhaw settlement in South Carolina in 1752. He served in the provincial militia in the campaign against the Cherokee Indians in 1760, entered the Revolutionary Army as captain of militia and attained the rank of brigadier general, commanded an expedition against the Cherokee Indians in 1782, became a member of the state house of representatives 1781-1794, was one of the commissioners named to settle the boundary line between South Carolina and Georgia in 1787, served as a member of the state constitutional convention in 1790, elected as an Anti-Administration candidate to the Third Congress (March 4, 1793-March 3, 1795), appointed major general of militia in 1795, and was a member of the state house of representatives 1800-1812. He died in Tomassee, Pendleton District,

S.C., August 11, 1817, and was buried in Old Stone Churchyard near Pendleton, S.C. (From Alice Noble's *The Fighting Elder: Andrew Pickens, 1739-1817.* Columbia: University of South Carolina Press, 1962.)

These are the ancestors that are your link for membership in the National Society of the Children of the American Colonists. Your Nina is a member of The Daughters of the American Colonists. Here is a list of how you fit into this branch of the family.

The Walkup-Pickens Connection

The list of ancestors on this side of the family in reverse order beginning with you, my grandson Williams McCain Kerr in 2015, and going back to 1724.

1. **Williams McCain Kerr,** born March 21, 1997, in Charlotte, NC. Son of James Maxwell Kerr

2. **James Maxwell Kerr,** born December 1, 1966, married Dana Michelle Atchley, May 20, 1995, born September 10, 1967, in Charlotte, NC. Son of Gladys McCain Kerr

3. **Gladys Elizabeth McCain**, born July 22, 1934, married James Donald Kerr, July 28, 1961, born January 19, 1934. Daughter of Robert Maxwell McCain, Sr., and Isa Winslow McCain

4. **Robert Maxwell McCain, Sr.,** born May 31, 1900, died December 22, 1984, married Isa Gladys Winslow, November 23, 1932, born August 28, 1903, died February 9, 1993. Son of Mary Elizabeth Walkup

5. **Mary Elizabeth Walkup** (b. Feb. 22, 1868-d. March 24, 1953), daughter of Israel Pickens Walkup, born April 9, 1826, died March 3, 1913, married (1st) Mary Isabel Harkey, 1856, born September 13, 1830-died January 1, 1881

6. **Israel Pickens Walkup(1826-1913)**, son of Samuel Pickens Walkup, born January 30, 1799, died 1885, married (first wife) Matilda Craig (first child was born November 26, 1820), died before 1833. Father of **Mary Elizabeth Walkup**, wife of Robert Thompson McCain

7. **Samuel Pickens Walkup (1799-1885),** son of Israel Walkup, born September 17, 1768-died October 6, 1827, married Margaret (Peggy) Morrow, March 5, 1795, born September 17, 1776 - died September 1, 1828

8. **Israel Walkup (1768-1827),** son of James Walkup (Rev. Capt.), born 1724 Pennsylvania, died February 1, 1798, Waxhaw settlement.

9. **Captain James Alexander Walkup (1724-1798)** born November 15, 1724, in Ireland-died February 1, 1798, in Old Lancaster, South Carolina (Waxhaw area). In 1757 he married **Margaret**

Nancy Pickens. Her grandfather was **William Henry Pickens** (b. 1670 LaRochelle, France-d. 1735 Lancaster, Pennsylvania) and her grandmother was Margaret Pike Pickens (b. 1672 Ireland-d. 1740 Bucks County, Pennsylvania). William had eight children born in Ireland and one son, Gabriel, who was born in Pennsylvania in 1715. William's son Israel Pickens was Margaret Pickens' father. NOTE: In 1811 the son of Andrew Pickens, Sr., who was the Revolutionary soldier Maj. General Andrew Pickens wrote the following letter to General "Light Horse Harry" Lee describing his family's movements from the time of his birth in 1739: *"I was born in PA, Paxton Township, on the 19th Sept. 1739. My father removed with his family when I was very young to Virginia, and settled for a few years west of where Staunton now stands about 8 miles, and in the year 1752 or 3, removed to the Waxhaws and was amongst the first settlers of that part of South Carolina. My father and mother came from Ireland. My father's progenitors emigrated from France after the revocation of the Edict of Nantes."* Maj. Gen. Andrew Pickens was the first cousin of Margaret Nancy Jane Pickens wife of Capt. James Alexander Walkup. Maj. Gen. Andrew Picken's father Andrew Pickens, Sr., and Margaret's father Israel Sidney Pickens were brothers.

What follows is an easy to read listing that shows how the Pickens, Walkup, and McCain families of the Waxhaw Settlement are connected and includes a complete list of children in each family.

The Pickens/ Walkup/McCain Connection

<u>**William Henry Pickens**</u> was born 1670 in La Rochelle, Manche, Basse-Normandie, France. Arrival in Pennsylvania in 1722 from Ireland. Died 1735 in Lancaster, Pennsylvania. He was the first of the Pickens to arrive in America. The records in Bucks County, Pennsylvania, from Neshaminy Presbyterian Church indicate that William Pickens and wife Margaret Pike Pickens were from Ireland and were admitted to the church in Neshaminy by certificate in April of 1720. William and Margaret were married 1692 in Ireland. His father was **Robert Andrew Pickens** b. 1644, Renfrewshire, Scotland; his mother was Esther Jeanne Bonneau, b. 1644, LaRochelle, France. Married 1660 Donaghmore, Tyrone, Ireland.

Children of **William Henry Pickens and Margaret Pike Pickens**

1. <u>**Israel Sidney Pickens,**</u> b. 1693, Antrim, Northern Ireland d. 1749, Cub Creek/Charlotte, Virginia. (Age 56 years)

2. Robert Pike Pickens, b. 1697, Limerick, Ireland -d. 01 Jun. 1793, Pendleton, Anderson, South Carolina

3. Andrew Samuel Pickens, Sr, b. 1699, Northern Ireland - d. 05 Nov. 1756, Anson, North Carolina (Waxhaw Settlement). *Father of Maj. Gen. Andrew Pickens (1739-1817) and cousin of Margaret Nancy Pickens (1740-1793)*

4. Thomas Pickens, b. about 1700-d. 1749, Augusta, Virginia

5. Anne Pickens, b. 1702, Tyrone, Northern Ireland -d. 1750, Waxhaw, Lancaster, South Carolina

6. Lucy Pickens, b. 1702, Ireland -d. 1762, North Carolina

7. William Gabriel Pickens, b. 1705, Ireland -d. 19 Nov. 1783, Montgomery, Virginia

8. John Pickens, b. 1710, Ireland -d. 1771, Pendleton, Anderson, South Carolina

9. Gabriel Pickens, b. 1715, Abingdon/Montgomery, Pennsylvania

Israel Sidney Pickens Family

Israel Sidney Pickens Born 1693 Antrim, Northern Ireland. In 1722 arrival in Pennsylvania. In 1726 married (1) Martha Davis b. 1708 in Ireland. Child. Anne Pickens b. 1726. Married (2) Martha Ann Nisbet b. 1710 Lincoln, NC-d. Oct. 1774 Gaston, NC. Children of second marriage were as follows:

1. William Pickens, b. 1728, Bucks, Pennsylvania-d. 1800, Mecklenburg, North Carolina

2. John Pickens, b. 1735, Pennsylvania-d. 1795, Grindle Shoals Bridge/South Carolina

3. Nancy Pickens, b. 1736, Augusta, Virginia-d. Abbeville, South Carolina

4. **Margaret Nancy Pickens** (1740-1793) SEE BELOW

5. Samuel W Pickens, b. 28 Apr. 1743, Charlotte, Virginia-d. 09 Jun 1821, Cabarrus, North Carolina

6. Jane Pickens, b. 1746, Charlotte, Virginia-d. 1781, Pendleton, Anderson, South Carolina

7. Rebecca Pickens, b. 1746, Charlotte, Virginia-d. 26 Oct. 1829, Tirzah/Mecklenburg, North Carolina

8. Hannah Pickens, b. 1749, Cub Creek/Charlotte, Virginia-d. 26 Oct. 1806, Charlotte, Mecklenburg, North Carolina

The Pickens/Walkup Connection

4. **Margaret Nancy Pickens,** b. 05 Mar. 1740, Augusta, Virginia-d. 22 Dec. 1793, Anson, North Carolina (Waxhaw Settlement). Married in 1757 **Capt. James Alexander Walkup** (b. 15 Nov. 1724) on ship crossing the Atlantic from Carrickfergus, Antrim, Northern

Ireland -d. 01 Feb. 1798, Waxhaw, Lancaster, South Carolina (Age 73 years). Children:

1. Samuel Pickens Walkup, b. 09 Oct. 1758, Waxhaw, Lancaster, South Carolina-d. 16 May 1851, Richmond, Madison, Kentucky (Age 92 years)

2. John Walkup, b. 06 Dec. 1760, Waxhaw, Lancaster, South Carolina-d. 12 Apr. 1823, Boone, Douglas, Missouri (Age 62 years)

3. James Walkup, b. 17 Sept. 1763, Mecklenburg, North Carolina-d. 30 Mar. 1784, Mecklenburg, North Carolina (Age 20 years)

4. Martha Walkup, b. 10 Feb. 1766, Mecklenburg, North Carolina-d. 03 Sept. 1820, Union, North Carolina (Age 54 years)

5. **Israel Pickens Walkup**, b. 17 Sept. 1768, Mecklenburg, North Carolina- d. 06 Oct 1827, Union, North Carolina (Age 59 years)

6. William Walkup, b. 22 Nov. 1770, Waxhaw, Lancaster, South Carolina-d. 01 Mar. 1859, Woodbury, Cannon, Tennessee (Age 88 years)

7. Agnes Nancy Walkup, b. 04 Dec. 1774, Lancaster, South Carolina- d. 25 Feb. 1831

8. Joseph Walkup, b. 22 Jun. 1776, Waxhaw, Union, North Carolina-d. 02 Apr. 1824, Mecklenburg, North Carolina (Age 47 years)

9. Robert Orr Walkup, b. 25 Jun. 1780, Waxhaw, Lancaster, South Carolina-d. 22 Sept. 1846, Mecklenburg, North Carolina

10. Margaret Walkup, b. 10 Aug. 1783- d. 28 Mar. 1860, Henry, Georgia (Age 76 years

Israel Pickens Walkup 1768-1827. Married Margaret Peggy Morrow, b. 11 Sept. 1776, Waxhaw, Union, North Carolina – d. 1 Sept. 1828, Waxhaw, Union, North Carolina (Age 51 years). Married 05 Mar. 1795. Bondsman James Baker, Witness James Wallis. Mecklenburg, North Carolina, Children:

1. James A Walkup, b. 17 Oct. 1795, Union, North Carolina-d. 23 Jun. 1874, Union, North Carolina

2. David Morrow Walkup, b. 14 Jun. 1797, Mecklenburg, North Carolina-d. 19 Aug. 1859, Yell, Arkansas (Age 62 years)

3. **Samuel Pickens Walkup**, b. 30 Jan. 1799, Mecklenburg, North Carolina - d. 16 July 1885, Jackson, Union, North Carolina (Age 86 years)

4. Syntha H. Walkup, b. 29 Oct.1800, Union, North Carolina-d. 13 Jul. 1820, Union, North Carolina (Age 19 years)

5. Martha P. Walkup, b. 22 Aug. 1802, Union, North Carolina-d. 08 Nov 1826, Mint Hill, Mecklenburg, North Carolina (Age 24 years)

6. Margaret Pickens Walkup, b. 17 Oct. 1804, Union, North Carolina-d. 07 Oct. 1875, Mint Hill, Mecklenburg, North Carolina (Age 70 years)

7. Elizabeth B. Walkup, b. 30 Dec. 1807, Waxhaw, d. 26 Sept.1881 (Age 73 years)

8. Nancy C. Walkup, b. Feb. 1809, Union County-d. 1900, Union, North Carolina (Age 90 years)

9. Anne Eliza Walkup, b. 29 Feb. 1812, Union-d. 05 Oct. 1905 (Age 93 years)

10. Israel H. Walkup, b. 11 Mar. 1813, Mecklenburg, North Carolina-d. 01 Sept. 1828, Mecklenburg, North Carolina

The Walkup/McCain Connection

Samuel Pickens Walkup 1799-1885. Married Martha Matilda Craig, b. 1805-d. 1844, North Carolina (Age 39 years). Several children including:

1. Samuel Harvey Walkup, d. 16 May 1892

2. Israel Pickens Walkup b. 9 April 1826-d. 2 March1913 m. Margaret Isabella Harkey 1/13/1829-1/1/1881. One of their children was **Mary Elizabeth Walkup** (1868-1953)

Mary Elizabeth Walkup 1868-1953 married **Robert Thompson McCain** (1860-1927).

One of their sons was **Robert Maxwell McCain Sr., 1900-1984**

Robert Maxwell McCain, born, May 31, 1900, died December 22, 1984, married Isa Gladys Winslow, November 23, 1932, born August 28, 1903, died February 9, 1993

Children of Robert Maxwell McCain and Isa Gladys Winslow McCain were

Gladys Elizabeth McCain Kerr

Robert Maxwell McCain, Jr.

Lelia Carole McCain Lewis

County Antrim (large circle above) is one of six counties that form Northern Ireland, situated in the north-east of the island of Ireland. It is one of six traditional counties of Northern Ireland and is within the historic province of Ulster from which many Scots-Irish Presbyterians including the McCains emigrated in the 1700's and settled in the Waxhaws along the North Carolina/South Carolina border.

Israel Pickens Walkup (1826-1913), father of Mary Elizabeth Walkup (1868-1953), the wife of Robert Thompson McCain (1860-1927)

Robert Thompson McCain

Mary Elizabeth Walkup McCain

Children and Grandchildren of Mary Elizabeth McCain (third from left above)

W.W. Walkup/Captain James Walkup Plantation House ,Waxhaw, NC

The McCains and Walkups were connected through the marriage of Robert Thompson McCain (1860-1927 and Mary Elizabeth Walkup (1868-1953).

The Walkups

(L-R)
Jenny Lynn Walkup Howard,
Uncle Sam (S.P.) Walkup,
Mary Elizabeth Walkup McCain,
Lee Walkup,
Charles Walkup, Sr.,
Buddy Boy Howard

Hugh McCain, Sr., and His Family

Now it is time to talk about your famous ancestor Hugh McCain, Sr. He is our ancestor for my Daughters of the American Revolution membership. Hugh McCain, Sr., was born in County Antrim, Ireland, in 1729 and sailed for America about 1752. He was red-headed and full of pep! He came to North Carolina with that band of Presbyterians from Pennsylvania who located and organized the Old Waxhaw Presbyterian Church. The McCains were among those people of Scotland and England who migrated to Ulster Plantation in Northern Ireland beginning in 1609. The migration was encouraged by James I who became King of England and Scotland in 1603 after the death of Elizabeth I. His goal was to establish a Protestant colony on land confiscated from Irish Catholic nobility. This was the beginning of conflict between Catholics and Protestants in Northern Ireland that endures even today.

By the 1690's the Protestants were in the majority in the province of Ulster, but because they were Presbyterians or other dissenters and not part of the Anglican Church, the official Church of England, they had few legal rights and were discriminated against. In 1703 the Queen Anne's Test Act caused further discrimination and large numbers of the Scots-Irish emigrated to the American colonies between 1717-1775. They often traveled together as entire groups of church members, relatives and neighbors. After five weeks or more on the Atlantic, they arrived in Philadelphia. They became farmers in Pennsylvania, but as population grew and land became scarce, they began moving in groups down an old Indian trail that became known as the Great Wagon Road. The settlers turned south from Lancaster and York, Pennsylvania, passed through Staunton and Lexington, Virginia, and into the Carolina frontier through Salem, Salisbury, and Charlotte. Beginning in 1751, they settled in the Catawba River valley of the Waxhaws along the remote North and South Carolina border on land abandoned by the Waxhaw Indians after the smallpox outbreak of 1741. The Waxhaw Settlement was named after Wisacky, the the tribal village of the Waxhaw Indians that had stood on the east side of the Catawba River. The wilderness land of the Waxhaws had a canopy of massive oaks and pines and grassy meadows and was advertised in New England and Europe as the "Garden of the Waxhaws." Often the settlers' 18 foot wagons served as homes until they could build log cabins. The Catawba Indians still lived nearby with whom there was often conflict. As a result, the settlers formed a close knit group for mutual protection and support and were suspicious of outsiders including Indians and non-Presbyterians. By 1760 there were more than 600 families living along Waxhaw and Cane Creek. The settlement was part of old Anson County until 1762 when the western section of Anson became Mecklenberg County.

Hugh McCain's first wife was Eleanor Nutt, the mother of all his nine children. Eleanor was the daughter of William Nutt (1705-1758) of Virginia. Eleanor died in 1789 and was probably buried in what is now an unmarked grave in the Old Waxhaw Presbyterian Church Cemetery between Waxhaw and Lancaster, SC. After the death of his first wife, Hugh married Jane Pickens Davis (1741-1820) who was a sister-in-law of General Pickens. Hugh McCain first lived on the eastern bank of the Catawba River at Landsford. The family was there only one year, for they were forced to flee for their lives due to the hostility of the Indians. For two years they lived at the Pink Neely place in North Carolina. They had many hardships and skirmishes with the Indians and soon moved to the Old Potter Road, turning southward, crossing into the fertile valleys of Cain Creek. They built a home on the hilltop above what is today named Cane Creek. Here they lived in peace and harmony until the American Revolution. Four of Hugh's sons, John, James, William, and Hugh, Jr., fought in the war. Your ancestor was Hugh's son Andrew.

Listen to this story about Hugh, Sr., as written by George T. Winchester: "With his boys all in the army and no banking facilities for the safe-keeping of his money, he, being old and tottering for the grave, decided that he could not protect it and decided he would bury it in the earth between his house and the creek. When the war clouds were breaking away about the time Cornwallis and his men were going back along this old Potter Road, hotly pursuing a band of foraging Tories who had heard of the old man's wealth, and these Tories found the old man out under a walnut tree. They captured him and demanded his money, but he refused to deliver the goods. They threatened his life by saying, 'If you do not surrender your gold we will hang you on the walnut tree.' They tied his hands behind his back and ran a noose over his neck, threw the rope over a limb and pulled him up but soon let him down and said, 'We will finish you the next time if you do not give up your gold.' He replied, 'I would rather suffer the tortures of the Brittians and die a martyr's death on the walnut tree than to surrender the gold that I have earned by the sweat of my own brow, as I have no desire to enrich the enemies of my country.' They pulled him up for the last time and tied the rope to a bush and he swung in the air. Then the old colored mammy servant named Tenor and her two boys caught on to the situation and came running and screaming at the top of their voices, and the Brittians, thinking it was Cornwallis' men, fled from the scene. Old Tenor and her boys cut the old man down and carried him into the house for dead, but he rallied and lived for two years. He lived to be ninety-three years of age, but his gold is still hidden so far as we know. He was buried in the Tirzah cemetery."

Hugh and his first wife Eleanor Nutt McCain had the following children:
Jane b. 1750 d. 1767
John S. McCain b. 10 December 1753, d. 9 March 1835,
William S. McCain b. 1756, d. 6 Apr 1823
(Often mentioned in the 1800 Diary of John Osborne)
Robert McCain b. 1757, d. about 1812
Hugh McCain Jr., b. 17 Nov. 1761, d. 19 May 1832
James McCain b. 1763, d. 16 Sept. 1827 - 1847
Andrew McCain b. 1769, d. 25 Nov 1845
Nutt McCain b. 1777, d. 14 Sept. 1814

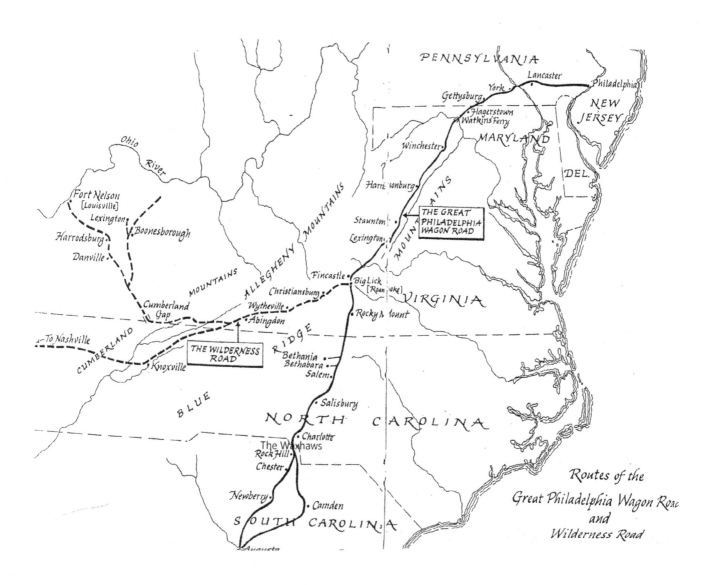

Map of the Great Wagon Road Used by Scots-Irish
and Others in the 1700's as They Settled
the Carolina-Virginia Frontier

Battle of the Waxhaws: A Brief Bibliography

"Battle of the Waxhaws" aka "Davie's Attack" was fought
on what is now Union County, NC soil on September 20th, 1780

✧

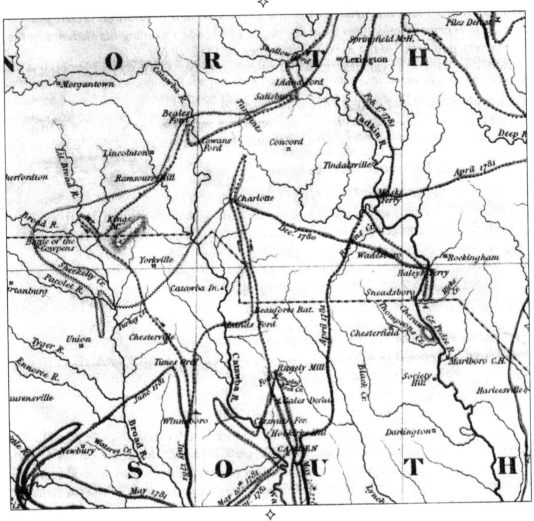

The Seat of War of the Revolution of the Southern States:
Shewing the Principal movements of the Hostile Armies
Engraved for Johnsons Sketches of the Life & Correspondence of Major General Greene
Published: 1822
Dates depicted: 1775-1783)
Creator: Henry Schenck Tanner (1786-1858)
Portion of map found at North Carolina Maps (UNC-Chapel Hill)-
http://dc.lib.unc.edu/u?/ncmaps,891

✧

Dickerson Genealogy & Local History Room
Union County Public Library
316 E Windsor St., Monroe, NC 28112

34

Name					
Brot forward	2168	2305	4305	63	1513
Charles Gillaspie	1	1	1		
John Haggins	1	1	1		
John Gillaspie	1	4	4		
Philip Kendrick	1		3		
John Hughey	1		6		
Samuel Lothlin	1		2		
John Lothlin	1		3		
James Lashy	1	2	3		1
Robert Lackey	1		2		
Thomas Lackey	1	3	3		1
Widow Lashy	2	1	1		
George Lowry	1	2	4		1
John McWhorter	1		1		
Hanson Myars	1	1	1		
John McElroy	4	2	2		
James McElroy	1	3	3		1
Moses McWhirter	1	2	5		
James McCorkle	1	4	2		
George McWhorter	3		2		
Owen McCorkle	1		2		
Andrew McCain	1	1	1		
Brice Mobley	1	3	4		
John McCain	1	1	2		
Hugh McCain	3	1			3
Thomas McCain, Junr.	1	3	1		
Drury Vinson	1	5	3		4
Jeremiah Washam	2	1	3		
Capt. Andrew Walker	1	1	6		3
John Williams	1	2	1		
James Withrow	3	2	3		9
Ishmael Williams	1	2	2		
John Walker	3		1		
Thomas Withrow	1	1	1		
Richard Griffin	1	3	1		
Barnabas Riddick	1	4	4		
Michel Oats	1	1	3		
James Brewster	2	2	3		5
Hugh Barnet	3	1	5		
James Black	2	3	5		
William Black Junr.	1		3		
Walter Baty	2	1	5		2
James Chambers	1	1	1		
Archibald Crockett	4	1	5		2
Roger Coningham	2	1	2		
James Currey	1	4	3		
Henry Davids	2				3
Samuel Davids	1		2		1
	2212	2390	4435	63	1544

Name					
Brot forward 383	2212	2390	4455	63	1544
Thomas Dunn	1	1	1		1
Robert Donelson	1	2	1		
John Guire	1	1	1		
John Guire	1	1	3		
Francis Hoge	2		4		
George Alckness	1	3	6		
George Hadden	1	2	1		
John Hodge	1	1	2		
David Houston	1	0	1		1
Isaiah Harrison	1	3	3		2
Daniel John	1	1	3		1
James McSpaven	1		1		
William Means	1	3	5		1
William McKee	1	3	2		6
John Miller	1	2	2		
Daniel McCauley	1		3		
Alexander McKee	1	3	4		
Phillip Moore	2	1	2		
George Montgomery	1	4	1		
David Moore Senr.	4	4	6		1
George Miller	1		2		
James McGughen					1
Alexander Morrison	2		2		1
William Wallace	1	8	1		1
Jesse Null	1	1	1		1
Andrew Null	1		2		
Robert Osborn	1		2		
Alexander Osborn	1	2	2		
Adam Osborn	1	1	3		
Abel Osborn	1		1		1
Moses Parks	3	3	3		
Simon Patton	2		3		
Gordon Potts	3	3	4		
John Patterson					1
Andrew Ray	2	2	4		
James Reid	1	2	4		
John Ray	1	1	1		
Joseph Reid	2	3	2		2
John Robison	1	5	3		2
David Ray	1	3	4		
Thomas Robison	1	2	5		
William Stuart	2		2		
William Plett	2	5	2		
Capt. John Simison	1	1	1		
James Shanks	1	1	6		4
	2270	2463	4528	65	1569

19

Ruins of the home of Hugh McCain, Sr. built in the 1750's and the old walnut tree from which the Tories threatened to hang him during the American Revolution.

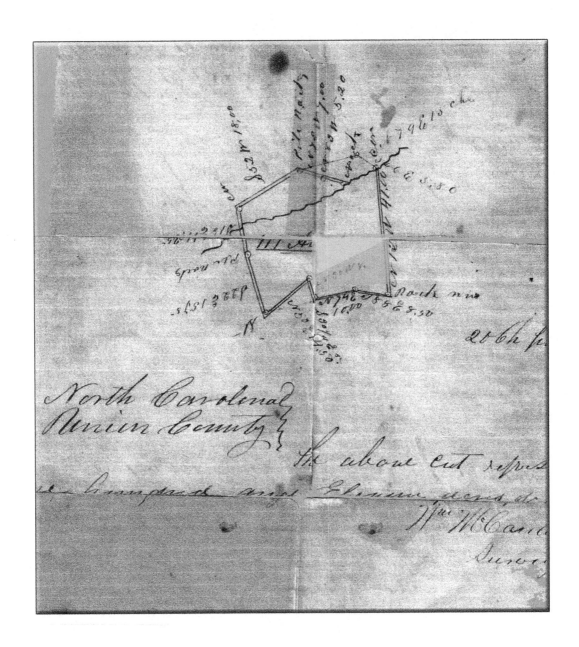

Plat of the land owned by Hugh McCain, Sr., located near Waxhaw in South Carolina in the 1750's, but after the boundary change of 1771 the plantation was in North Carolina. What remains of the old homestead is on a hilltop southeast of Cane Creek and what is today Providence Road, NC Highway 16. The plantation included what is today Union County's Cane Creek Park.

The tombstones of Hugh McCain, Sr., and his second wife Jane Davis McCain (L) and Robert Thompson McCain and his wife Mary Elizabeth Walkup McCain (below) in the old cemetery at Tirza Presbyterian Church, Waxhaw, North Carolina

Hosea McCain 1860 Mecklenburg County Census

SCHEDULE 1.—Free Inhabitants in _____ in the County of _____ State of _____ enumerated by me, on the 19th day of July 1860. _____ Ass't Marshal.

Post Office _____

821 / 411

		The name of every person whose usual place of abode on the first day of June, 1860, was in this family	Age	Sex	Color	Profession, Occupation, or Trade of each person, male and female, over 15 years of age.	Value of Real Estate	Value of Personal Estate	Place of Birth, Naming the State, Territory, or Country.	Married within the year	Attended School within the year	Persons over 20 y'rs of age who cannot read & write	Whether deaf and dumb, blind, insane, idiotic, pauper, or convict.	
1	2	3	4	5	6	7	8	9	10	11	12	13	14	
186	186	John W. Belk	33	m		Farmer	800	4000	N C					1
		Elizabeth	30	F		Taylor			"					2
		Elenor	7	F					"			1		3
		Mary Etta	5	F					"			1		4
		Samuel R.	3	m					"					5
		George W	½	m					"					6
		Britton	16	m		Farm Laborer			"			1		7
187	187	Hosea McCain	66	m		Farmer	700	300						8
		Nancy	52	F		Domestic								9
		John C.	26	m		Farmer			"			1		10
		Harriett	18	F		Domestic			"			1		11
188	188	Thos W Sanders	50	m		Farmer	1000	500	S C					12
		Ann	45	F		Domestic			New Jersey					13
		Ann	12	F					N C			1		14
		Jacob	14	m					"			1		15
		Jennett	6	F					"					16
		Obediah M	2	m					"					17
189	189	Noah Sanders	20	m		Farmer		300	"			1		18
		Mary	20	F		Domestic			"			1		19
		Frances	1	F					"					20
190	190	Dixon Spray	51	m		Farmer		800	"					21
		Elizabeth	51	F		Domestic			"					22
		John	32	m		Farm Laborer			"					23
		Robinson	24	m		"			"					24
		Jefferson	22	m		"			"					25
		Samuel	21	m		"			"					26
		Mary	18	F		Domestic			"					27
		Tabitha	16	F		"			"					28
		Emily	13	F					"			1		29
191	191	William Godfrey	30	m		Miller		200	"					30
		Charity	18	F		Domestic			S C					31
		Elizabeth	6	F					N C					32
		William	4	m					"					33
		Josephine	1	F					"					34
192	192	William E McCain	28	m		Farmer	800	3500	"					35
		Margaret	20	F		Domestic			S C					36
		Sarah	22	F		"		2000	"					37
		John J.	18	m		Farmer	800	2000	"					38
193	193	G C Godfrey	27	m		Farmer	800	300	"					39
		Margaret A	18	F		Domestic			"					40

No. white males, 20 No. colored males, _____ No. foreign born, _____ No. blind, _____ 3,800 / 13,900 No. idiotic, _____

No. white females, 20 No. colored females, _____ No. deaf and dumb, _____ No. insane, _____ No. paupers, _____ No. convicts, _____

1910 Census Union County, NC Listing the Family of Robert Thompson McCain

The family of Robert Thompson McCain and Mary Elizabeth Walkup McCain 1904
(Back L-R) Samuel Hosea McCain, Mary Elizabeth McCain, Ella Jane McCain
(Front L-R) Myrtle Walkup McCain, Robert Maxwell McCain, Mary Elizabeth McCain.
Robert Thompson McCain, Connie Lee McCain (baby), Granny Mary McCain Simpson

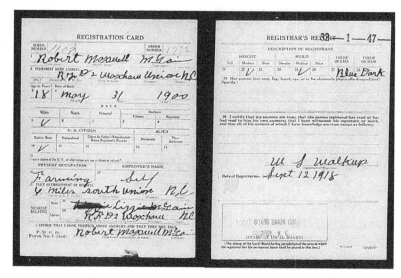

World War I
Draft Card of
Robert Maxwell McCain,
son of Robert Thompson
McCain

Winslow Sisters: Lessie, Novella, Mary, Eunice, Mama, Aunt Mary, Aunt Ruth, Aunt Sadie

Cousins Bill, Bob, and Arnold

Granddaughter Gladys McCain

Children of Mary Elizabeth and Robert T. McCain

Uncle Knox McCain

Knox, Maxwell, Connie, Grandson Bill,
Uncle Joseph Winslow

Granny's brother Joe Walkup with
sisters Addie Neal and Nettie Huey

Mary McCain Simpson, grandmother
of Robert Maxwell McCain (1860-1927)

Isa Gladys Winslow McCain and husband
Robert Maxwell McCain, Sr.

Gladys Elizabeth McCain Kerr and son James Maxwell Kerr

FARMERS GINNING AND TRADING COMPANY, INC.

BOX 236   ...   PHONE 843-2169

GENERAL MERCHANDISE, FERTILIZERS, FEEDS, AND SEEDS

W A X H A W, N.C.   2 8 1 7 3

Annual Statement of Business done by
Farmers Ginning & Trading Company, Inc.
December 31, 1970

Assets

Cash on hand	$ 2,698.63	Capital stock	$ 8,050.00
Cash in bank	7,305.84	Notes payable	1,000.00
Stock Merchandise	11,884.30	Bill payable	4,560.37
Accounts receivable	8,894.35	Taxes payable	807.38
Notes receivable	2,293.04	Interest payable	160.00
Gin plant	346.87	Undivided profits	20,153.19
Land	200.00	Capital surplus	980.00
Frozen food box	531.28	Profit	739.91
Warehouse	136.24		
Air conditioner	453.20		
Drink box	690.90		
1964 Truck	1,016.20		
	$36,450.85		$36,450.85

Farmers Ginning and Trading Company Annual Statement 1970 and retirement letter of Maxwell McCain, Treasurer

FARMERS GINNING AND TRADING COMPANY, INC.

BOX 236   ...   PHONE 843-2169

GENERAL MERCHANDISE, FERTILIZERS, FEEDS, AND SEEDS

W A X H A W, N.C.   2 8 1 7 3

August 10, 1973

Directors
Farmers Ginning and Trading Company, Inc.
Waxhaw, North Carolina

Gentlemen,

As acting manager of Farmers Ginning and Trading Company, I am submitting my resignation to become effective September 1, 1973. Due to my state of health and age, I feel this is the appropriate time to retire.

It has given me great pleasure and satisfaction to serve the Farmers Ginning and Trading Company for forty-seven years.

Yours truly,

Maxwell McCain

Maxwell McCain

The Old Meeting House of the Waxhaw Settlement and cemetery at Tirza Presbyterian Church where many of the McCains are buried including Hugh, Sr. Gladys McCain Kerr is pictured inside the Meeting House.

Eleanor McCain b. 1779

The second wife of Hugh McCain, Sr., was Jane Pickens Davis (1741-1820). Hugh McCain and his wife were active in the old Waxhaw Presbyterian Church between Waxhaw and Lancaster, SC, and later in Tirza Presbyterian Church near Waxhaw where he is buried. His will of 1805 listed his seven sons and one daughter. He divided his plantation between sons and appointed his son Hugh, Jr., as one of the executors.

Next, we need the generations that connect you to Hugh McCain, Sr. Here is the list.

The McCains of Waxhaw, NC

Hugh McCain, Sr., born in County Antrim, Ireland, in 1729, died August 26, 1821, married 1) in 1747 Eleanor Nutt (1733-1789) mother of all his children, married 2) Jane Davis, born 1741, died June 24, 1820, buried beside her husband in Tirzah Cemetery. It has been said that Hugh McCain, Sr., was an Ensign under George Washington at Braddock's Defeat. It was reported all these McCains had libraries. The parents of Hugh McCain, Sr., were most likely **Robert /Alexander McCain** (1703-1789) of County Antrim and Sarah Hamilton. Robert McCain lived and died in York, Pennsylvania. His son Hugh lived in Pennsylvania before moving with other settlers to the Waxhaws in the 1750's. (It is not know for certain whether Hugh McCain was born in Ireland and moved to America with his parents or was born in York, Pennsylvania.)

Andrew McCain born 1765 or 1769, (DAR papers say ca. 1770) died November 25, 1844 or 1845, married Mary McKee (Montgomery) (first wife) and Mary Grimes (second wife); moved to Missouri. Another source says his birth date was 1857 and he lived in the Waxhaw area.

Hosea McCain, third child of Andrew, born July 14, 1794, died May 19, 1878, married Susannah Harkey (first wife), Nancy C. Walkup (second wife) Hosea was father of John J. and John W. (Wheelwright)

Alexander Maxwell McCain born October 8, 1820, died July 29, 1861; married Mary Huey McCain, died July 29, 1848 (first wife) married Mary Elizabeth McCain (second wife) c. 1850, born January 9, 1837, died June 24, 1919. Mary Elizabeth married David Simpson, born May 10, 1819, died September 26, 1865, after Alexander Maxwell was kicked by a mule or horse and died. Alexander Maxwell taught school in Union County, NC in 1850.

My grandfather, **Robert Thompson McCain**, son of Alexander Maxwell McCain, born April 24, 1860 died June 11, 1927; married Mary Elizabeth Walkup, February 7, 1884, born February 22, 1868, died March 24, 1953

My father, **Robert Maxwell McCain**, born, May 31, 1900, died December 22, 1984, married Isa Gladys Winslow, November 23, 1932, born August 28, 1903, died February 9, 1993

Gladys Elizabeth McCain Kerr, your grandmother, daughter of Robert Maxwell and Isa, born July 22, 1934, married James Donald Kerr, July 28, 1961. He was born January 19, 1934

Your father, **James Maxwell Kerr,** son of Gladys and Don Kerr, born December 1, 1966, married Dana Michelle Atchley, born September 10, 1967. They were married May 20, 1995.

And finally you, **Williams McCain Kerr,** born March 21, 1997. This is your McCain lineage. Below is an interesting copy of the Last Will and Testament of your ancestor Andrew McCain:

The Will of Andrew McCain

*I, Andrew McCain of Union County, North Carolina being of sound mind but considering my mortality and knowing that it is appointed for all men to die considering it my duty to settle my estate touching worldly things do make and publish my last will and testament in the following manner and form and first I resign my body to the earth and my spirit to God who gave it. I allow all my Just debts and funeral expenses paid out of my Estate. I give and bequeath to my wife Mary during her life my house and plantation provided she choose to live on it also my boy Plato and one of my girls her choice also my waggon three head horses Hornet my sorrel filley and any other she wishes my Blacksmith tools farming tools sufficient for her use six head of cattle hogs and sheep as many as necessary also my house hold and kitchen furniture as much as she may wish and also my loome my books to remain with her during her life and then by Equally divided amongst my children. I allow my wife to have the disposal of one bed and furniture as she pleases the ballance of the property at her death to be equally divided amongst all my children by Sale or otherwise as my EXRS may thing best. My will is that Jane Steele and Martha Carraway have first out of my Estate forty Dollars each in lieu of a horse and John W. McCain and Eleanor Harkey account for the negroes they have received and then take an equal division with the rest E. Harkey three hundred and fifty dollars & J. W. McCain agreeable to his note. My will is that my girl Nicy to go to Jane Steele or any of my children she may choose without any division or expense to the rest the balance of my Estate real and personal I allow to be sold and equally divided amongst all my children but if the rest of my negro girls wish to remain amongst my children they have the privilege to choose a master. I appoint John Stewart & J. W. McCain Exers of this my last will & testament and revoke all former wills by me made.
Signed sealed published and acknowledged by me this 5 day of October one thousand eight*

hundred and forty four in presents of us witnesses.

Andrew McCain (SEAL)

George McCain
J. M. Stewart
William McCain
State of North Carolina, Union County
*   Court of Pleas & Quarter Session July Term 1845*
*   The last will and testament of Andrew McCain (Deed) was exhibited in open court and was proven in due form of law by George McCain & J. M. Stewart two of the subscribing witnesses thereto and ordered to be recorded.   Will Book 1 Page 10   Hugh Steward CCC*

Memories of My Grandparents:
Mary Elizabeth Walkup McCain and Robert Thompson McCain

For years, my only vacation was to spend a week or two with my Granny McCain at Route 2, Waxhaw, NC. The house where my Daddy was born was her home since she was sixteen and married Grandpa. Grandpa Bob bragged about that pretty Walkup girl who rode her horse sidesaddle. To a friend he said, "See that girl on the horse, I am going to marry her." Their farm and home were located on Harkey Road, now the location of Cane Creek Park.

My youngest McCain cousin and youngest granddaughter, Lynn McCain Twitty, is the youngest child of Uncle Knox and Aunt Ruth. Lynn had two older brothers, Bill and Arnold. Uncle Knox and Aunt Ruth, from the day they were married until death, lived with Granny in her house. Lynn was only five years old when Granny died. I was a freshman at Flora Macdonald College. I cut Saturday classes to come home. I felt so sad for Daddy, and I really loved my Granny. I asked Daddy if I could go to Uncle Knox's and spend the last night with them before the funeral. Lynn only remembers Granny's body was brought home and placed in the parlor before the funeral. Bill and Arnold have both died as I write this family history. I am so sorry I never asked them for stories. They would have had numerous good ones since they lived with Granny. Granny Lizzie and Grandpa Bob (Robert Thompson McCain) had nine children, two died as babies. Those who survived were Aunt Mary, who married Uncle Berge Norwood; Uncle Sam, who married Aunt Kate Haigler; Aunt Ella Jane who married Uncle Mahlon Helms; Aunt Myrtle who married Uncle Kirk McCain; my Daddy, Robert Maxwell who married Isa Gladys Winslow; Uncle Connie who married Aunt Sadie Carter; and Uncle Knox who married Aunt Ruth Starnes. Granny and Grandpa were loyal members of Tirzah Presbyterian Church, the oldest or one of the oldest churches in Union County. Grandpa was church treasurer and treasurer for the Bible Society. They are buried in the Tirzah Cemetery with the two little babies. I have asked permission to have my foot stone placed in their plot. My son, James, will see to this.

Here is an Uncle Sam story my Daddy told me. Of course all the boys-Sam, Maxwell, Connie, and Knox- had to farm with Grandpa Bob. It seemed that for some reason Uncle Sam just did not sweat! At lunch time one day, Grandpa Bob seeing Sam's shirt was dry, not wet with sweat, assumed he had been playing or goofing off! Sam got a terrible whipping. The next day before coming home for lunch, Sam jumped into the Davey Lake so he would be wet all over!

Now an Uncle Connie and Daddy story: Daddy was such a tease; he told Uncle Connie to put two bales of fodder under his arms and jump from the barn loft. Uncle Connie was told he could fly. Needless to say, this did not happen. Daddy was unjustly punished for throwing rocks one Sunday as Aunt Myrtle built a play house. One of the boys told Grandpa Bob, Maxwell was playing ball on Sunday. A whipping followed without investigation of the facts.

Before I was in high school Robert, my brother, and I spent a week or two with Granny Lizzie during our summer vacation from school. We also were invited to Aunt Ella Jane's and Aunt Myrtle's homes for a few days. Bennett, Aunt Ella Jane's baby, was about my age. Aunt Myrtle had three boys: Dale, Harry Lake, and Joe. She also had the dearest daughter, Mildred, who though much older than I, was indeed one of my very favorite cousins. Her daughter Jeanne took piano lessons from the same teacher I had, Mrs. Sarah Walker. Aunt Myrtle had a pump organ in her living room. How I enjoyed playing it, and I so wanted it to be mine. I feel sure Jeanne has it now. Lake and Joe teased me badly, but it was all in fun. The meals at all my relatives' homes were "out of this world." There was country ham, fried chicken, numerous vegetables from the garden, and always pie or cake!

Without question Sundays meant Sunday school at Walkersville. I recall the Sunday School Building was a large room with just curtains to separate the classrooms. I made new friends and saw numerous cousins. A bountiful lunch, called dinner back then, followed. Many Sundays Granny Lizzie and/or Uncle Knox would invite the preacher and his family to come for dinner.

At Granny Lizzie's house there was a separate building for storing the cotton and the cotton seed. What fun to jump in the soft, fluffy cotton, but it was not too much fun to have to pick the cotton. The sun was hot and the rows seemed very long. A cool drink of water and an occasional breeze were ever so welcome! Usually my job was to deliver cool water in fruit jars to the field for the men. I liked staying on the back porch with Granny, trying to help prepare vegetables for dinner. I continue to be amazed that we did not get sick from eating food left on the table, covered with a table cloth only. The flies were sometimes bad! Do you know what fly paper is? Some stores and homes used it. It was a long, curly strip of sticky paper which was hung from the ceiling. It did catch lots of flies. Taking a full bath was a rare event, but each night there was a pan of water, soap and a rag placed on the porch facing the cow barn, which meant: wash your dirty feet before going to bed. I heard Mama say many times when they came to take me home that it appeared I could use a GOOD BATH.

The entire McCain Clan came to Granny Lizzie's for her birthday, February 22nd. Never did I see so much food. The house was small, the dining table looked like it might collapse. There was an abundance even after all were fed. The adults always ate first and the children played in the yard until we were called in to fix our plates. The iced tea was so good.

Granny Lizzie was a very small woman who weighed about 100 pounds, and she was about five feet tall. She had only one blood brother, Samuel Pickens Walkup. Uncle Sam had a General Store at the SC line on Providence Road. There was a gas tank in the yard, a porch on the front of the building, a rocking chair for whomever, and his house was in the yard, a big rambling one-story structure. The old store is still standing but no longer in use. I visited Uncle Sam's youngest son, Charles Henry Walkup, who was a cousin, and dear, Eloise, his daughter. Eloise helped me tremendously with the founding of the Piano Scholarship at Wingate University in memory of our piano teacher, Sarah Chapman Walker.

Back to Granny: She always wore an ankle length dress, usually one Aunt Ella Jane or Aunt Mary sewed for her. Her colors were drab: gray, black, or some black and white small design patterns. She wore a long slip and black stockings. Her shoes were oxford style, about an inch and a half heel, always black. Since I had to share a bed with Granny when I visited, I knew she wore her bra on top of her slip, imagine! Shh…I do not think she wore panties. She was a very private, quiet lady, but with definite opinions. Mama sometimes felt Granny thought she might be a bit extravagant! Granny's hair was thin and gray, but it never turned completely white like mine. She wore it up on top of her head in a tiny ball. When she was younger, she parted her hair in the middle and pinned a ball on the back of her head. Oh, how I loved my Granny. She let me help her churn butter on the side porch next to the cow barn. This is the porch on which I washed my feet in a pan of water each night before going to bed. Granny's bed had a feather tick on top of the mattress. You sank way down in and felt warm and safe. There was no inside bathroom, but Granny had a chair with a hole cut out in the middle with a potty on a shelf below. It was my job to take the potty to the outhouse each morning, yuk. But it was great not to have to go out in the dark to use the pot.

Not only did I get to churn, but Granny taught me to "string green beans" and shell peas. I never cooked. I could wash dishes in a dish pan. She had a "safe," cabinet structure, where she kept flour and meal: large bins of flour and meal. The country hams were hanging on rafters in the smoke house, wrapped in burlap. The sausage she canned in quart jars. Irish potatoes, onions, sweet potatoes, and jars and jars of pickles, fruits, and vegetables were stored on earthen shelves in the cellar. The trap door to the cellar was just outside the cow barn porch. It was dark and cool down there. I was very afraid to go down those steps! My Granny's favorite desserts were cherry pie and banana pudding. You see, her birthday was the same as George Washington's, February 22nd, therefore, cherry pie! Mama always made one or both when Granny came to eat with us. Granny had this thing about being back home before dark, or never going anywhere when it was storming! Not a bad idea, probably.

Most of Grandpa Bob and Granny Lizzie's children joined Walkersville Presbyterian Church after having gone to Tirzah for many years. Granny never moved her membership from Tirzah. She always invited her circle to meet at her house in August so she could serve watermelon.

Uncle Sam Walkup must have sold children's clothes as well as gas, fertilizer, and groceries because one of my cousins said Granny bought several of the granddaughters a pair of under panties from the store. Maybe it was Myrtle Norwood Simpson who told me this story. Perhaps Geraldine, Cooper, and Mildred got the gifts, and Myrtle was overlooked.

I think I mentioned Charles Henry Walkup, Uncle Sam's son who was a good friend of my Daddy. Uncle Sam had a daughter, Ginny Lynn, who married Oliver Howard. The Howards had a plantation, maybe a grant from the King of England. Ginny Lynn's house still stands on Providence Road near Rea Road. She showed me a mantle clock that Granny Lizzie had given her for a wedding present. I so wanted her to give me the clock but it never happened.

Don't tell, but Granny dipped snuff! "Railroad Mills" brand. She carried her little tin box of snuff in her apron pocket. She was never seen without her apron, unless she was on the way to church. She had me to go break a little green twig so she could use it as a brush to dip her snuff. She had a tin can into which she would spit. Never was she untidy or messy with this snuff. I never wanted to try it! She did let me drink a little coffee with lots of milk and sugar. I liked that. When Granny drank coffee she poured it into her saucer and sipped it from the saucer rather than drinking from the cup!

Granny must have made a million quilts. You see she had to make all her children's clothes and as they wore out, she saved the scrapes to make quilts. I think she also made those feather beds we all slept on when we were small. They were made from goose feathers. When my Daddy got married, Granny gave him his feather bed. I kept it a long time, and then I gave it to my son, James. She wanted me to quilt. She kept her quilting frame up in the living room during the winter months. She cut me a pattern and helped me get started with my squares. To this day I have that little bag of quilt squares, but no quilt! Granny always read the *Christian Observer*, a church paper, sitting in her little rocker, without arms, by the open fireplace.

If grandchildren were at Granny's house, and we got too loud, or we were not working hard enough, she would address us as, "You chaps, stop that fighting, being loud, or whatever." Sometimes she called us "youngins."

I keep thinking about the house in which my Daddy was born, and the only home my Granny Lizzie had after her marriage to Robert Thompson McCain. It was never painted and had a tin roof. There were four porches: the front porch where Granny sat each Sunday afternoon watching for Daddy to drive up in the big truck, the side porch facing the cow barn where I washed my feet in a pan each night, the side porch facing the mule barn where Granny and I shelled beans and peas, and the fourth porch sort of facing the road was where we played. Aunt Ruth worked in the field, and I carried water to the field. Robert and I spent each summer with Granny until we were in high school. I am remembering my sister Carole going with Robert and me to Aunt Myrtle's one summer, and she got homesick and all three of us had to return home.

I also spent part of my summer vacation with Uncle Connie and Aunt Sadie. Maybe Robert came along with me. Flora was a little older than I, but we both loved playing the piano. Bobby was my age. Aunt Sadie made the most delicious Canadian War Cake. It had fruit, nuts, and caramel icing. Bobby told me a story about the cat getting into a cake Aunt Sadie had cooling on the back porch. My dear cousin, Flora, married and had two lovely daughters, Debbie and Sherry. When her son Mitchell was born, she had a blood clot and died. What a tragic situation. Flora's sister Mary helped with the three children. I believe Mama told me Mary also baby sat with Robert and me when we were children. Years later, Debbie's daughter Erica took piano lessons from me.

When Granny died my freshman year in college, I asked to spend the last night before the funeral with Uncle Knox and Aunt Ruth. Flora Macdonald College had Saturday classes then and I missed a Trig quiz and received a zero. Professor Ellie Mae Sowder did drop your lowest score, and that had to be mine! Daddy was Executor of Granny's will. All the sons got land, but not Daddy. Daddy bought the Twitty Place which joined Grandpa Bob's farm. I think Daddy told me he allowed Aunt Ella Jane and Uncle Mahlon to live in the Twitty house. When Robert went to UNC Chapel Hill, Daddy sold the Twitty Farm because two of us were in college for several years at the same time. Robert was runner-up for the coveted Morehead Scholarship at UNC Chapel Hill.

Now for some stories my cousin Robert Lee McCain, Uncle Connie's son, shared with me. On March 8, 2014, Bob told me these stories about Grandpa and Granny.

1. Bobby says our grandpa was a man of faith, a leader in the church, and treasurer of the Tirzah Bible Society. Grandpa was a good farmer and a strict disciplinarian. It is said he was bad to whip the boys. He was a good carpenter and blacksmith. His blacksmith shop was across the road from the house and near the grape vines. He built several of the farm buildings located near his house. I believe he may have built his house, too. How efficient he was: he could shoe horses, sharpen tools and knives, construct door hinges, plow parts, fireplace tools, and other needed items. He taught his sons to be blacksmiths.

2. Uncle Connie got 5 cents from his Pa at the end of each week. One week Pa gave him a different coin. Uncle Connie refused to accept the coin because it was a different size from his regular nickel. Pa took it back and gave him a nickel. "Boy you do not know the value of money." Uncle Connie had refused a quarter!

3. R. T. McCain had the best watermelons and took these to Bible Society at Tirzah. Remember, Granny served watermelon to her ladies circle when they came in August.

4. Grandpa was about to sell his horse, Trueboy. He told Uncle Connie to ride to the top of the hill and let him rip coming down. A dog bit the horse on the nose and threw Uncle Connie in the road, but the buyer purchased Trueboy anyway.

5. Once Uncle Connie was angry with one of his brothers or sisters and refused to come to supper. Grandpa gave him a good whipping. Truly Connie loved all his brothers and sisters.

6. Uncle Connie and Uncle Knox were supposed to be walking to church at Walkersville.

They skipped out and went to the saw mill and several other stops. Grandpa learned about each stop and rattled them off as he proceeded to whip them soundly.

7. Grandpa had a hired boy named Berge Anthony who lived upstairs in the smoke house. Uncle Connie took him his breakfast each day. One day Connie loosened the steps on the stairs and when he called Berge to get his breakfast, of course he fell. Grandpa said if Berge Anthony was crippled, then Connie would have had to do his work and Berge Anthony's as well!

8. Grandpa sent Uncle Connie and Berge Anthony to gather fodder. The weather got colder and they built a fire in the field. They sat down in the field just to talk. They were caught, whipped and poor Berge's shoe had a hot coal inside which he was not allowed to shake out. He worked that day with a burning foot!

9. Uncle Connie wanted to use the cradle to cut grain. Grandpa said, "No, you could get hurt." But Connie took a wide swing and cut his finger. He wrapped the bleeding finger in his handkerchief and worked all day, wounded. By the way, I gave Uncle Sam Walkup's cradle to the Museum of the Waxhaws.

10. Uncle Connie was forever throwing rocks in the yard. One day he found a piece of glass, threw it, and hit one of Granny's Guinea hens in the top of its head. It flopped and flopped, and died.

11. Uncle Connie taught his dog Trixboy to kill snakes. He would catch a snake, make it strike at him, and when the snake stretched out, the dog would shake him and break the snake's neck. The dog was smart to grab the snake in its middle section to shake it.

12. Grandpa Bob bred horses; he kept some and sold some. He had a mare named Maude and a colt named George. Horses in the Jackson area were known as a team. These two horses worked together better than anything they had seen. Connie told onlookers they could pull a wagon load of hay and corn from the bottom land. The horses pulled until they gave out and fell to their knees. "Get Up." "Pull Again."

13. Grandpa told one tenant to go "lay by" the watermelons and plant peas. How do you do this? The tenant saved one vine that was so pretty. I do not understand this picture, but I shall try to reproduce it as Bobby told me: You reverse the pile of dirt, like so...

My grandpa had a history of mental illness and spent his last days in the asylum in Morganton, NC. He was overseer of the farm for the facility. He did get better and could have returned home, but he refused. He was afraid he might relapse or even unintentionally hurt someone. The family visited him as often as possible, and I now own some letters my Daddy wrote to Grandpa while he was in Morganton.

Walkerville Presbyterian Church Honors Robert and Elizabeth McCain

Some years ago Walkersville Presbyterian Church honored my grandparents. I am copying some of the material the church used on that Sunday. I do believe Mama and I went to this service.

"*Today we honor the Robert Thompson and Mary Elizabeth Walkup McCain Family. Mr. R.*

T. McCain owned a farm on Harkey Road at Cane Creek Park. He was a good farmer and also did blacksmith work to keep the farm equipment in good repair. He was a strong disciplinarian as sons Connie and Knox witnessed when they skipped church one Sunday to play at a saw mill. Mr. R. T. was known for his good crops; however, one of his "plow hands" misunderstood his instructions one summer and plowed up all of his watermelon vines except for one. Mrs. McCain, known affectionately as "Aunt Lizzie" or "Cousin Lizzie," is pictured by her family and friends as a "fixture" on the front porch with her tattered, well-read Bible, fly swatter and quilting material. Her grandchildren found her blackberry jelly and biscuits irresistible. They also liked to receive her "brownies" (pennies) for running errands for her. She loved Tirzah Bible Society meetings and believed in strict observance of the Sabbath Day. Robert Thompson McCain had seven children who lived---four boys (Sam, Maxwell, Connie, and Knox) and three girls (Mary, Ella Jane, and Myrtle). Although all the children are now deceased, two daughter-in-laws remain and live in our community. Maxwell's wife, Mrs. Isa Winslow McCain, lives on Raymond Helms Road with her daughter Gladys Kerr, and grandson James Kerr. Knox's wife, Mrs. Ruth Starnes McCain, lives on Harkey Road at the "home place." Mrs. Ruth is a faithful member of Walkersville Church along with her daughter and son-in-law, Lynn and Boyet Twitty, Jr. and their children, Allison and Todd.*

Other descendants of the R. T. McCain family who attend Walkersville Church are Mrs. Geraldine Brady, Rhonda, Terry, and Tarah McManus; Cathy, Krista, and Kayla Swinson; Hazel, Sarah, Neely, Brian, and Kelly Simpson; Bob and Jo Nell McCain; David and Pam McCain; Beverly, Dean, and Lauren Haney; Debbie, Dennis, Erica and Neil Robinson; and Mitchell, Pam, and Adam Gordon.

Robert Thompson McCain and Mary Elizabeth McCain: Children and Grandchildren

My grandfather Robert Thompson McCain was born April 24, 1860, and died June 11, 1927. My grandmother Mary Elizabeth Walkup McCain was born February 22, 1868, and died March 24, 1953. They married February 7, 1884. Granny was 16 and Grandpa was almost 24. Seven children of this marriage lived. Two babies died and are buried in the old Tirzah Cemetery, where James will bury my ashes.

1. **Mary Margaret Elizabeth McCain** Norwood (Born August 30, 1885) (Died June 10, 1972). Married to Alphonzo Berge Norwood (Born January 8, 1884) (Died November 10, 1949). Married November 6, 1907. Seven children were born to this marriage, four boys and three girls.

2. **Samuel Hosea McCain** (Born May 27, 1890) (Died March 28, 1968)
Kate Elizabeth Haigler McCain (Born June 14, 1892) (Died June 16, 1970)

Married December 28, 1909. Three children were born to this marriage, 1 boy and 2 girls.

3. **Ella Jane McCain Helms** (Born May 28, 1893) (Died January 23, 1981)
Mahlon Alexander Helms (Born June 24, 1888) (Died July 16, 1968)
Married January 10, 1910. Seven children were born to this marriage, 4 boys and 3 girls.

4. **Myrtle Walkup McCain McCain** (Born October 17, 1897) (Died June 7, 1982)
James Kirk McCain (Born September 13, 1892) (Died December 1, 1961)
Married December 6, 1916. Four children were born to this marriage. 3 boys and 1 girl.

5. **Robert Maxwell McCain** (Born May 31, 1900) (Died December 22, 1984)
Isa Gladys Winslow McCain (Born August 28, 1903) (Died February 9, 1993)
Married November 23, 1932. Three children were born to this marriage. 1 boy and 2 girls.

6. **Connie Lee McCain** (Born July 1, 1903) (Died March 14, 1990)
Sadie Roxanna Carter McCain (Born June 21, 1908) (Died August 13, 1962)
Married February 22, 1927. Three children were born to this marriage, 1 boy and 2 girls.

7. **Knox Ratchford McCain** (Born May 29, 1907) (Died August 21, 1979)
Ruth Mae Starnes McCain (Born December 27, 1913) (Living). Married February 25, 1933. Three children were born to this marriage, 2 boys and 1 girl.
Below are stories and background information on the families of each of the children of Robert and Mary Elizabeth McCain beginning with their first child Mary Elizabeth.

Mary Elizabeth McCain Norwood Family

On Sunday, September 28, 2014, Phonzo and Clara Starnes, the grandson of Aunt Mary, came to see me. They brought a grand picture of them for my Granny Lizzie book. Phonzo told me he worked for Daddy one summer at the Farmers' Store. Daddy had asked him to shuck some of the corn he had in a basket at the front of the store. He did the job quickly and reported for the next task. How glad Daddy was to have a young man who really wanted to work! Phonzo thought there was a Post Office in the store, but that structure was Daddy's office. Phonzo remembered some Massey fellow coming in the store for cigarettes and questioning the price he quoted. The customer insisted Mr. Maxwell gave him a special price. Phonzo did the right thing by asking the gentleman to see Mr. Maxwell. Sure enough for whatever reason, Daddy did let him have the purchase at a discount.   Clara is getting me names and birthdays for Aunt Mary's children. How grateful I am to them.

Phonzo Harrison Starnes, son of Brascus Harrison (Jack) Starnes and Cooper Elizabeth Starnes, was born December 5, 1942. He married Clara Joan Hallman Starnes, August 18, 1968. Clara was born September 27, 1945. They have two sons: Chad Starnes, born October 26, 1975, and Seth Harrison Starnes born November 20, 1977. Clara taught school for about 20 years, and she is now retired. Cousin Albert Starnes, grandson of Aunt Mary McCain Norwood and son of Cooper Norwood Starnes, is a great story teller.

Albert and his wife Hazel have been wonderfully kind to me, not just with this story of our grandparents, but with many of my civic responsibilities. Al took time to visit on Thursday, August 28, 2014. The purpose was to take a look at my book, up to this point. He was encouraging and shared several stories about my parents. Al thinks his son Bo will be interested in the book, and he said he would pay the cost for publishing one copy. I am thrilled he wants a copy.

Now, not only did he tell me a story or two, but he promised to contact Norwood cousins to get birth dates, death dates, and possibly some pictures. I look forward to receiving this information. Aunt Mary was a charmer; a true Southern Lady, loved to dress tastefully, and she always wore her jewelry! Her hair was beautiful, long and thick, and she wore it on top of her head in a precious ball! I loved when she came to visit us in Waxhaw. Al told me his grandmother really liked my Mama. He went on to say, "Aunt Isa always did things in the right and proper fashion." Mama indeed insisted flowers be on the table, a lovely cloth, usually made by her, napkins, china, and proper table settings to greet our guests. Her Mother, Lelia, had taught her well, and I try to continue her hostess instructions.

Time for another story: This one involves the characters Aunt Mary, Albert, his brother, Phonzo, and their cousin, Walker. Cooper and Nellie were working and Aunt Mary was in charge of these three grandsons. Most of the time, they played well together, but Walker could not hear nor speak, and sometimes this made him feel "inferior" or "left-out." One day he was out of sorts with Al and Phonzo, and he did a mean thing. He caught two of Aunt Mary's hens and one rooster and threw them down the hole in the "out house." Aunt Mary was angry, of course, but Walker told it was Albert and Phonzo that did this awful deed! Jack Starnes, the boys' father, "wore them out." Just like boys, right? Well, the end of the story is that years and years later during a Norwood Reunion, Walker's wife told Al, Walker had a confession to make. It seems all those years, Walker regretted blaming his cousins for the chicken tragedy. He asked for "forgiveness." You see, Jack Starnes not only whipped his sons, he made Albert fetch the chickens from the toilet pit. He provided Al with a bent coat hanger and instructions for rescuing the birds. The chickens did not like being pulled and tugged, and they flapped their wings in protest. You know the rest of the story; Albert was covered from head to toe with stinky stuff! How did he ever get clean? I hope he forgave Walker.

During the 1950's, Albert worked for my Daddy at the Farmers' Store. One of his jobs was to load feed or fertilizer from an upper shelf storage area to the back door. Instead of lifting each bag separately, he was pushing them from the shelf to the floor. Daddy caught him doing this with the very last bag. Albert got a Maxwell lecture about the cost prohibitive situation of causing any one of the bags to burst! Albert knew better; he was just being a little lazy! No more pushing seed or feed bags onto the floor! Daddy even mentioned it might cost one a year's salary to cover the loss! Daddy was a true Scotsman; watch every penny!

William Davis was working at the store while Albert was employed. William's father, Mr. Will Davis, had stock in the business and had clerked there himself. Albert felt William was not motivated to be a salesman. William had to be prodded to dust, sweep, or stock shelves. He had a bad habit of staring at customers! Albert said he thought my Daddy told William just to hold a broom and look like he was contemplating sweeping! Albert said William told him the store did not belong to my Daddy. This really bothered Albert, and he went home to ask his parents about that statement. William was correct. The Farmers' Store was owned by a group of stock holders, my Daddy included. Daddy even bought stock for his three children. Daddy was manager and treasurer, and as far as I am concerned, IT WAS HIS STORE. Without my Daddy at the helm, it would never have succeeded.

Albert and my brother, Robert, were both interested in athletics, especially baseball and basketball. When I see Albert and Hazel, he always inquires about Robert. An amusing sideline he shared was about teaching the young people at Bethlehem Methodist Church to dance. The ruling body called a meeting to tell him this action was not acceptable. The hurt from this attack encouraged Albert to start attending Unity ARP Church in SC. Things do work out for the best: Albert now had an opportunity to get to know Aunt Myrtle and Uncle Kirk's family. He became close to and admired Joe, Aunt Myrtle's baby boy. Mildred, Dale, Lake, and Joe were all active members of Unity Church. See, blood is thicker than water!

Granny Lizzie's Walkup family lived in the Unity Community where Aunt Myrtle lived. Albert keeps in contact with Charlie Buck, Charles Henry's son. Charlie Buck took piano lessons from Mrs. Sarah Walker, just as I did. He is extremely talented. Albert was unusually kind and thoughtful of Charlie Buck's crippled sister, Eloise. Eloise loved ball games, but she walked with crutches or was in a wheel chair. Albert told me he took her to all the basketball and baseball games at Parkwood High School. Her father, Charles Henry Walkup, never went to bed until Albert delivered Eloise home safely. Albert said Eloise would not take the easy way ever. She insisted on coming down a number of steps from the front porch, and she refused help from Albert. "I can do it myself."

Shortly after my Daddy retired from the Farmers' Store, William Davis attempted to operate the business. This failed and the building became a home for a restaurant. Albert and Hazel owned the restaurant for a time. The menu was hamburgers, hotdogs, and ice cream! Hazel fired Albert several times because he was in charge of the ice cream sales, and if a child had only 4 cents, not a nickel, he allowed him or her to have ice cream regardless! You know, I bet my Daddy would have done the same thing! Update: Albert has followed up by contacting his cousins about my book. They seem interested. He invited me to the Norwood Reunion this September, but I cannot go. Maybe they will invite me next year.

Another story about Cooper, Ellen Belk, and Cooper's boys: Cooper, Albert, and Phonzo were invited to Ellen's home for Tea. All the way to Lancaster, Cooper instructed her boys: smile, be polite, eat and drink whatever is served. Several other ladies were

The Oldest Daughter of Robert Thompson McCain

Mary Elizabeth McCain Norwood and husband Alphonzo Berge Norwood

An early photography of
Mary and Berge Norwood
with their children Rob and Ellen

The Granddaughter of Robert Thompson McCain:
Myrtle Norwood Simpson and husband Simmie Simpson

Phyllis Simpson Garner and husband Gerald Garner

Benjamin Garner

Ashley Garner Blackon and husband
Nathan with twins Carter and Caroline
and daughter Charlotte

Holly Simpson Garner and husband Jason with son Zach

Bill Norwood and wife Ruth

Cooper Norwood Starnes
and husband Jack Starnes
with children Albert,
Phonzo, and Libby

Class of 1937 William (Bill) Norwood back row second from right

(L-R) Bill Norwoood's wife Ruth, Franklin, Bobby, Billie Ann, Rick Norwood

Bill's son Franklin Olen
and wife Lynn

Bill's daughter Billie Ann
and husband Harry Hicklin

Three Children of Cooper and Jack Starnes

Son Albert Starnes and wife Hazel

Daughter Cora Elizabeth (Libby) and husband Charles Edward Kiser, Jr.

Son Phonzo Starnes and wife Clara

Walker and Jane Norwood,
Rob and Nellie's son

Several Descendents of Andrew McCain attended Unity School (1901
Photo. Kirk McCain is first row number four from left. Unity is located
between Waxhaw, NC, and Lancaster, SC.

invited and it was time for tea. Albert said he had never had hot tea, only iced tea. The cups were tiny and the crumpets looked like little dog biscuits, but he smiled and ate and drank as he was instructed by his mother. Ellen's husband Paul Baker was an engineer for Springs Mills. Ellen allowed me to use her papers when I applied for membership in Daughters of the American Colonists. Their daughter Dannie has been in education for a number of years. I attended Ellen's funeral in Lancaster some years ago. There are so few first cousins still living.

McCain, today is Tuesday, September 9, 2014, and my mind is restless. A family in my church is facing the consequences of apparent money laundering and fraud from illegal business transactions. They have been my friends for a long time, and I feel so sad and disappointed about this news. I can and will pray for justice to be done. Nevertheless, this news made me even more aware of the lessons my parents taught me about responsibilities, work ethics, dependability, and honesty. To my knowledge, neither of my parents ever knowingly took advantage of anyone, nor was there any effort to cheat in business relations. At the store, my Daddy would go the second and third mile to assist a customer or friend when necessary. He never owned but two automobiles, a green Chevrolet and a blue Dodge Dart. He paid cash for these cars, for he did not believe in using credit cards or being in debt to anyone. For a short time, he had a Texaco gas card, which he got rid of in short order. It was not his style! When Daddy died in 1984, he was not in debt to any person or business. He owned stock in the store and in the American Bank and Trust Co. He had a savings account. He and Mama divided the monthly bills between their two social security checks, so the electric, fuel, telephone, and tax bills were paid on time. How they ever managed to send me, Robert, and Carole to college is a miracle. The three of us tried to help financially by working summer jobs, working on campus, and taking advantage of some scholarship money. Robert worked one summer for a concrete company in Charlotte. He came home so hot, tired, and dirty. Another summer he worked for the Allied Van Moving Company at their warehouse in Washington, DC. I worked for Woolworth Dime Store in Charlotte, Belk Department Store, and Cato Clothing in their warehouse. Carole had an office job for a construction company, I believe. "A good name is rather to be chosen than great riches." I am so grateful for loving, caring parents who taught us by example.

Samuel McCain Family

I need more information about Uncle Sam and Aunt Kate. I well remember Uncle Sam farmed on the same side of the road where Uncle Knox lived. Aunt Kate was a Haigler. They had three children: Mary Lee, Geraldine, and Harold. Harold and his wife, Mary Lee Gordon McCain, lived with Uncle Sam and Aunt Kate. They had one daughter, Jane, about my sister Carole's age. Jane died tragically in a car wreck. Later Harold moved to Monroe and took his Mom and Dad with him. Mary Lee made beautiful afghans. Uncle Sam's daughter, Mary Lee, married a Chandler and had three children, two girls

Samuel and Kate McCain Family

Sam and Kate McCain with daughter Mary Lee
1912

Mary Lee Gordon McCain
wife of Harold McCain

Sam Hosea McCain 1890-1968 and wife
Kate Haigler McCain 1892-1970

Harold McCain 1916-1961
son of Sam McCain

Geraldine McCain Brady and Family
Front Row: Rachel, Mary Lee McCain, Geraldine McCain Brady, and son Lamar

Dean, Harold, Mary Lee, Lamar, and Lou

Geraldine's son Melvin Brady

Emily, Melvin, Dean, Lamar, Mary, and Lou

Beth, Lamar, Fanny Mae, Tracy

Melvin, Dean, Cy, Lou, and Lamar

Wedding of Rachel and Melvin Brady's Daughter Cathy
Melvin, Rachel, Kayla, Cathy, Hollis Gordon, Krista, Hallie Gordon

Wedding of Melvin's granddaughter Kayla
(L-R) Rachel, Cathey, Kayla, Cam, Kristi, Colton

Grandmother McCain and Her Children 1951

Tarah, Terry, and Rhonnda McManus
Uncle Sam's Great-Granddaughter

Emily's Family: Granddaughters of Uncle Sam and Aunt Kate

and a boy. She died at a fairly early age. Geraldine married a Brady and had three sons. Melvin, her oldest son, at one time farmed my land where I continue to live. I do believe all three boys have died. Geraldine's granddaughter Rhonda Brady McManus lives nearby and her daughter Tarah took piano lessons from me. Tarah was extremely talented and Geraldine was very proud she played so beautifully. Tarah practiced on Geraldine's piano. Maybe Rhonda will be able to tell me more about Uncle Sam's family. Geraldine shared flowers and plants from her yard when I built my house on Raymond Helms Road. She also talked with me about Granny and Grandpa McCain. She shared some pictures which I cherish. When I was in rehab with my knee replacements, Geraldine was living in the same facility, Jesse Helms Center in Monroe. We ate some of our meals together and I tried to walk down and visit with her from time to time. I truly loved this gentle, kind lady.

February 28, 2015

McCain, Rachel Gordon Brady graciously agreed to ride with me to find Mary Lee McCain Chandler's daughter, Mary Pettus. She was not home, but we met her daughter Lisa, and Lisa's daughter Courtney. Lisa and Mary have lovely homes just off of Providence Road South, really quite near me. Mary lives with her son, Stephen, and Mary's sister Emily Chandler Massey lives in Monroe. Later in the day Mary phoned me and said she and Emily would come to see me to learn more about the stories and pictures I am collecting for you. Lisa told me a little about her memories of Aunt Kate McCain, who would be her great-grandmother. When she was small and visited Aunt Kate, they would make biscuits together. Lisa loved Aunt Kate's long hair, which she penned up in a bun. I also remember how welcoming Aunt Kate and Uncle Sam always were. She was indeed a splendid cook!

Rachel came to identify pictures Wednesday, March 25, 2015. She shared this story about the birth of Uncle Sam and Aunt Kate's second child, Geraldine. "The year was 1914 and the month was March. There was snow on the ground. It was time for the baby to be born. Uncle Sam bravely rode his horse to Sapp's Cross Road to fetch the doctor. Dr. Sapp arrived in his buggy and delivered a beautiful baby girl on March 8, 1914." Dean was always one of my favorite cousins: so kind, loving, helpful, and a lover of flowers. April 7, 2015: McCain, I stopped to visit with Bob and Jo Nell after I worked for your Dad in his office today. Bob had a few good stories about Uncle Sam which I want to relay to you. It seems Uncle Sam was quite the fisherman! The story goes that he could dig a hole in the middle of a corn field, fill the hole with a bucket of water and them pull out a fish! At one time Uncle Sam was breeding hybrid catfish in his pond. The fish watched for him to come bringing bread to feed them. Another tale involves the Brown's Mule Plug Chewing Tobacco he so enjoyed. Bill, Arnold, and Bob worried him about wanting to try that chewing tobacco. When Uncle Sam gave in and the boys took a chew, all three of them got really ill. I bet that was the last "chew" for them. At another time, Uncle Sam was hauling a hay frame on a wagon and the frame turned over landing Uncle Sam flat on his back.

Ella Jane McCain (Helms) Family

McCain, it is March 16, 2015. Lynn Rogers Stikeleather has sent the best pictures and several written documents about her grandmother Ella Jane and family. These are her memories: "Ella Jane McCain Helms was my grandmother. I called her Granny. She was born May 28, 1893. She was the third child of Robert Thompson McCain and Mary Elizabeth Walkup McCain. She had four brothers and two sisters: Mary Margaret Elizabeth, Samuel Hosea, Myrtle Walkup, Robert Maxwell, Connie Lee, and Knox Ratchford. A few months before her seventeenth birthday she married Mahlon Alexander Helms on January 9, 1910. They had seven children: Lucille Elizabeth, Elise Catherine, Robert Ralston, Mary Margaret, Eugene Clayton, Thomas Lee, and Charles Bennett. Mary Margaret was my mother.

Granny was an attractive, reserved lady, a little on the portly side. She was always dressed neatly in a dress or skirt and blouse. For church or funerals, she wore a suit, hat, gloves, and dressy shoes. Her everyday shoes were black leather, lace up with about a 2 inch heel. They did not cover her ankles or look comfortable. The stockings she wore were held up with elastic garters. She rolled the top of the stockings around the garters and positioned them just above her knees. Sometimes late in the day when she was tired, she rolled them down around her ankles. As a child who didn't like shoes anyway, I wondered why she didn't just take her shoes and stockings off. I think she preferred the privacy of her bedroom. I am not sure if I ever saw her bare feet.

The first home that I remember Granny and Grandpa living in was located on highway 200, a few miles south of Monroe, North Carolina. They lived several other places before they moved there. It was a nice home with a screened in porch on the front and one side. Chinaberry trees grew in the front yard. There were two ponds a little distance from the house. Inside, Granny always kept it clean and without clutter. The furniture was well taken care of and looked nice. One of the beds had a wooden headboard that almost reached the ceiling. The footboard was about half as high. In the kitchen, Granny baked delicious damson plum pies. There was a damson plum bush near the house where we picked the plums. Her cornbread smelled so good cooking and tasted great with her stewed potatoes. Granny and Grandpa's personalities were very different. She was much more serious. He was always smiling and didn't seem to have a care in the world. When they were together, he did most of the talking. She always called him Nick instead of Mahlon. I don't know where that came from.

When my Uncle Gene lived in San Bernadino, California, my Aunt Elise took Granny and Grandpa to visit him. They had a wonderful time and spoke often of the things they saw and did. They brought back a lot of souvenirs that Granny placed around the house. Most were breakable and we weren't allowed to touch. Later when my Uncle Gene moved to Ocala, Florida, they visited him there. Mama went with them. That was an enjoyable trip also. Sometime in the late 1950's, Granny and Grandpa moved to Charlotte, North Carolina. They lived down the street from my Uncle Thomas and his family and my Aunt Elise and her family. They were very happy there.

When Grandpa was diagnosed with brain cancer in 1967, Mama started spending more time with him and Granny. She worked in Waxhaw, North Carolina during the week and stayed with them in Charlotte on weekends. My daddy, Claude Rogers, died of kidney cancer on February 17, 1966. He was 49 years old. Mama was a young window at age 47. She decided to quit her job and move in with Grandpa and Granny. She found a job close by their home and helped with his care at night and on the weekends. Grandpa died on July 16, 1968. After his death Mama moved to Monroe, North Carolina. Granny stayed in Charlotte, but did move across the street from my Aunt Lucille and her family.

Granny had a good relationship with her siblings. She always spoke highly of them. She enjoyed visiting with Aunt Myrtle, Uncle Connie, and Uncle Max and Aunt Isa. Sometimes the visits lasted a week or more. She always felt welcome, especially with Uncle Max and Aunt Isa. For the most part Granny lived a healthy life. In the late 1970's, she developed congestive heart failure. This illness would take her life on January 23, 1981, at the age of 87. She was preceded in death by two of her children, Gene in 1972 and Margaret, my mama, in 1975."

Each of the children of Mary Elizabeth Walkup McCain and Robert Thompson McCain named a son after their father:

Mary ...Robert Wilson
Sam...Robert Harold
Ella Jane...Robert Ralston
Myrtle...Robert Dale
Maxwell...Robert Maxwell
Connie...Robert Lee
Knox...Robert Arnold

Listing of family members of Ella Jane McCain Helms

Ella Jane McCain was the third surviving child of Robert Thompson McCain and Mary Elizabeth Walkup McCain. Ella Jane was born May 28, 1893, and died January 23, 1981. Her husband was Mahlon Alexander Helms (Born June 24, 1888) (Died July 16, 1968). They were married January 10, 1910. They had four boys and three girls.

Their fourth child was **Mary Margaret Helms Rogers** (Born August 18, 1918) (Died December 31, 1975). Married to Claude Guion Rogers (Born October 27, 1916) (Died February 17, 1966). Married August 24, 1940.

Two children were born to this marriage, one boy and one girl:

Larry Guion Rogers (Born August 31, 1941) (Died September 20, 1979) m. Mary Zeta Perrell Rogers (Born December 5, 1941). Married October 14, 1961.

Ella Jane McCain and Mahlon Helms Family

Mahlon Alexander Helms

Ella Jane McCain Helms

Early Helms family portrait

Ella Jane's sons: Ralston, Gene, Thomas Lee, and Bennett

C.J. and Lynn Stikeleather's Family.

Uncle Maholn and Aunt Ella Jane with
grandchildren Diane Helms, Ernie Creech

C.J. and Lynn Stikeleather's
50th Wedding Anniversary

Children of C.J. and Lynn Strikeleather:
Christi, Jay, Lisa, Ginger

Everette Oliver Sparks
7th Generation of Robert Thompson
McCain Family, son of Emily Sparks

Noah Evans and Anna Kate Frye,
Children of Ashley Matthews Frye

Larry Rogers' Grandchildren:
Ashley Frye, Phillip Matthews,
Woody Poston, Alex Poston,
Kayla Croft and Kelsey Croft

Larry Guion Rogers son of Margaret
Rogers and Grandson of Ella Jane

Ella Jane and Mahlon (R) with Claude and
Margaret Helms Rogers (Larry's Parents)

(Left Back Row)
Uncle Mahlon,
Elise, Aunt Ella
Jane, Alexander
Weddle (Lucille's
husband), Lucille,
Margaret, Libby,
(Benny's first
wife), Benny and
Thomas (Front R)

Aunt Ella Jane and Uncle Mahlon Family

Lynn, Mary, Jean, Thomas (holding Diane), Margaret, and Elise about 1951

Grandchildren of Aunt Ella Jane and Uncle Mahlon

Margaret Rogers' daughter Lynn and C.J. Stikeleather's Family

Aunt Myrtle and Uncle Kirk's Family

Larry Rogers' daughters Dana Croft,
Amy Matthews, Cheryl Mims,
Beth Poston

Aunt Ella Jane's descendants Mary,
Jerry, Lucille, Jane, Ann, Sarah

Ella Jane's son Benny Helms
and wife Judy

Sixth Generation of Granny Lizzie's Family (Children of Paige and Matthew
Norwood): Mattie, Hali, Emma, Presson, and Peyton

Matthrew and Paige Stubbs Norwood

McCain Carlone

Kathy Helms Stubbs

Aunt
Ella
Jane
McCain's
great-
grand
children

Stratton Stubbs

Thomas and Jean Helms 40th Anniversary

Diane Helms
Countryman,
Debbie Helms,
Thommy Helms

Vince and
Cynthia Stubbs
Carlone

Bill Helms, Grandson of Ella Jane McCain

His Wife Peggy Perry Helms

Their Son David Helms

Their Daughter Laurie Helms

Note: After Larry Rogers' death his wife Zeta married Franklin Isgett who adopted the the four girls of Larry Rogers and Zeta.

Amelia Jane Rogers Isgett Matthews (Born May 16, 1962),
>   m. Kerry Mark Matthews (Born October 7, 1963) who married March 9, 1985.
>   Two children were born to this marriage, one girl and one boy:
>   Ashley Erin (Born September 20, 1986)
>   m. Matthew Scott Frye (Born January 15, 1988). Married September 30, 2013.
>>   two children were born to this marriage, one boy and one girl:
>>   - Noah David Evans (Born February 19, 2010),
>>   -Anna Katherine Frye (Born August 19, 2014)
>   Phillip Mark Matthews (Born September 29, 1989)

Mary Beth Rogers Isgett Poston (Born December 26, 1963)
>   m. Harrell Linwood Poston (Born November 4, 1963) who married
>   January 15, 1983.
>   Two children were born to this marriage, two boys:
>   Harrell Linwood Poston, Jr. (Born April 7, 1991) and
>   Alexander Wilton Poston (Born June 2, 1993)

*Cheryl Renee Rogers Isgett Mims (*Born August 2, 1968).
>   m. Steven Ray Mims (Born February 6, 1961) Married May 26, 1995

Dana Denise Rogers Isgett Croft (Born January 14, 1970)
>   m. Kenneth Harold Croft, Jr. (Born September 23, 1968)
>   Married September 19, 1992
>>   Two children were born to this marriage, two girls.
>>   Kelsey Elizabeth Croft (Born October 1, 1994)
>>   Kayla Marie Croft (Born October 12, 1999)

Nancy Lynn Rogers Stikeleather (Born December 29, 1945)
m. Clifford John Stikeleather, Jr. (Born July 31, 1945)
Married January 3, 1964
Five children were born to this marriage, three girls and two boys.
> 1.Lisa Jon Stikeleather Moore (Born August 21, 1964)
> m. Troy Alexander Moore (Born October 25, 1963)
>   Married September 8, 1984
>   Three children were born to this marriage, two girls and one boy.
>>   Emily Jon Moore Sparks (Born May 26, 1987)
>>   m. Christopher Allen Sparks (Born May 20, 1988)
>>   Married March 16, 2012
>>   One child was born to this marriage, a boy.
>>   Everette Oliver Sparks (Born February 5, 2015)
>>   Grant Alexander Moore (Born May 13, 1989)

Carley Jane Moore (Born January 17, 1995)
2. Christi Lynn Stikeleather Hearne (Born January 24, 1966)
  m. Frank Douglas Hearne (Born August 2, 1966)
  Married June 18, 1988
  Four children were born to this marriage, two girls and two boys.
    Mason Douglas Hearne (Born April 23, 1991)
    Madison Lynn Hearne Crawley (Born August 11, 1992)
    m. Michael Andrew Crawley (Born November 30, 1990)
      Married October 12, 2013
    Mackenzy Jane Hearne (Born January 13, 1994)
    Mahlon John Hearne (Born April 14, 1996)
3. Ginger Ann Stikeleather Couick (Born March 5, 1967)
  m. Howard Scott Couick (Born July 20, 1970)
    Married December 7, 1991
  Five children were born to this marriage, one girl and four boys.
  Chelsea Ann Couick (Born July 20, 1992)
  David Seth Couick (Born September 30, 1994)
  Noah John Couick (Born May 28, 1996)
  Nathan Scott Couick (Born January 27, 1998)
  Josiah Gentry Couick (Born May 14, 2002)
4. Jason Guion Stikeleather (Born January 26, 1974) (Died January 26, 1974)
5. Matthew Jay Stikeleather (Born May 11, 1975)
  m. Laura Diane Calderon Stikeleather (Born March 1, 1978)
  Married October 7, 2000
  Three children were born to this marriage, one girl and two boys.
    Joselynn Diane Stikeleather (Born December 18, 2003)
    Camden Jay Stikeleather (Born January 18, 2006)
    Matthew Justus Stikeleather (Born November 23, 2007)

Myrtle McCain McCain Family

The following information regarding Aunt Myrtle and Uncle Kirk was provided by their son Harry Lake McCain. When Uncle Kirk was courting Aunt Myrtle, he came calling in a buggy drawn by a horse. Aunt Myrtle lived long enough to see men walk on the moon! When the WPA was active in their community, Uncle Kirk used his mules and wagon to haul dirt. He said the horse and mules brought more money than he was paid. I was told he had two mules and one horse.

Lake became a soldier on December 19, 1944. After 16 weeks of basic training, he was

Aunt Myrtle, Aunt Mary, Uncle Connie, Maxwell, Ella Jane

Myrtle and
Kirk McCain
Family

Myrtle McCain

Uncle Kirk and Aunt Myrtle

Uncle Kirk and his mules

Row 1: Roger, Betty, Shawn, Karen. Row 2: Jeannie, Rosemary, Aunt Ada, Aunt Eva, Margie, Betty, Joseph. Row 3: Joe Ewart, Ross, Mildred, Lake, Dale, Michael

Aunt Myrtle

James Kirk McCain

Myrtle and Kirk McCains' Sons: L-R Lake, Joe, Dale

Mildred Kirk McCain
born 1919

Ross C. Hinson born 1911
Husband of Mildred

Son Lake McCain
World War II

Myrtle, Joe Ewart, Glen Dale, and Jimmy

Joe Ewart, Myrtle, and Harry Lake

Aunt Myrtle

Front: Mildred and Joe, Back: Lake and Dale

Mildred and Joe Ewart

home on furlough. While he was home, President Franklin D. Roosevelt died and Harry Truman became our president. Lake was stationed in the Philippines and was scheduled for the invasion of Japan. He credits President Truman with saving his life by making the tough decision to drop the Atom Bomb. His older brother Robert Dale, exactly two years and ten months older, was a Marine. His younger brother, Joe Ewart, was a soldier stationed in Germany. How about all three of Aunt Myrtle and Uncle Kirk's boys being in the military! We McCains love our country and are proud to defend it against all enemies.

Lake and his wife Betty had two children, Karen and Roger. Roger had two children by his first wife and one daughter, Morgan, by his second wife. Roger lives in Greenville, SC, and Karen, who has two daughters, Bailey and Chandler, lives on Neal Road in the Unity Community. Chandler was married recently (2015).

My cousin Karen, Aunt Myrtle's granddaughter, told me a story about her grandfather Kirk: "He died when I was four and a half, but my special memory is when Dad would get home from work in the afternoon and we would jump in the car and go to Granddaddy's house. Granddaddy would throw open the back door on the screen porch and throw his arms out saying, 'Come here my little ones or my grand youngens.' We would then hang out while Daddy worked in the garden, or I would ride the mule Mary while Daddy plowed. I believe that squash was Grandmother Myrtle's favorite vegetable in the garden, and she always had squash in some fashion. She also saved coffee grounds and egg shells as garden fertilizer. Daddy told me that when I was born, he came home from the hospital and went over to Grandmother's to tell everyone. Uncle Mahlon was there and said, 'Poor man's luck, bull calves and baby girls.' I guess I showed him! Every Sunday morning Mom got Roger and me up and dressed, and we went with Daddy to Grandmother's to pick her up to take her to church. After everyone had their Sunday afternoon naps, we would all gather under the big oak tree in front of their house and go over the world and community news. You were not a McCain grandchild until you fell over the tree stumps and skinned a knee. We took many, many trips down the bank on whatever we could find."

Another story, McCain: Rosemary found the most wonderful pictures of Aunt Myrtle and Uncle Kirk. There was a wonderful picture of their three sons. When I returned the originals, I had a visit with Betty, Joe Ewart's wife. I asked her a few questions and discovered Joe was most probably born, not at home, but in a hospital of a sort in Lancaster. If there were a boss in this family, it was probably Aunt Myrtle. They did not take vacations to the beach or mountains, but Uncle Kirk would ride the train to New Jersey to visit his sister. When the family met him at the deport, maybe in Waxhaw, his first question was: "How are my mules?" Early in the Unity Community, there was surely a one-room school. Later a fine school was built at Buford. I think Mildred worked in the cafeteria; maybe ran it! The first Unity ARP Church broke off from Tirzah, which was also ARP and changed later. I knew Aunt Myrtle made quilts, but Betty told me she loved to make Baby Quilts for young mothers. Her favorite pattern may have been the Dutch Girl. Betty's son John was blowing leaves and he expressed a desire to have copies of some of

Rosemary's pictures. How helpful my family is with this project! I so love my McCains!

CHRISTMAS 2014: DEATHS OF TWO COUSINS

BURWELL WINSLOW DIED ON DECEMBER 9, 2014. BURWELL WAS UNCLE PERCY'S BABY BOY. HE WAS ABOUT THE AGE OF YOUR NINA, McCAIN. HIS DAUGHTER, CATHY, HAS BEEN A TREMENDOUS HELP WITH GRANDMOTHER LELIA'S BOOK. CATHY SENT ME THE OBITUARY.

HARRY LAKE McCAIN DIED ON DECEMBER 24, 2014. LAKE WAS THE SON OF AUNT MYRTLE AND UNCLE KIRK. HE LIVED IN THE UNITY ARP COMMUNITY, AND WE HAD SOME TIME TO REMEMBER CHILDHOOD HAPPENINGS DURING THE PAST YEAR. I TALKED WITH LAKE'S DAUGHTER, KAREN BAXLEY, A FEW TIMES. I TOOK COOKIES AND SAUSAGE BALLS TO HER HOME. I LEARNED SOME GOOD STORIES ABOUT LAKE AT HIS FUNERAL, WHICH WAS HELD AT UNITY ARP CHURCH ON DECEMBER 28, 2014.

McCain, You can chuckle at some of these happenings!

Lake was in the Army during World War II. He was stationed in the Phillipines and later was sent to Japan. He said it was not the atomic bomb that scared the Japanese, but the thought that he was coming after them! Lake believed in working hard and in a responsible manner. "If you do not work, you do not eat." It seems he borrowed a sum of money from Uncle Knox McCain to build the house where he was living up to the time of his death. The interest was 6% and he paid the loan off in short order. He never went in debt again. "If you don't have it in your back pocket, you do not need it."

Soon after his first wife Betty died, he married a lady he had known when he was much younger. Millie was welcomed by the Unity Community. Some teased Lake about marrying so soon after Betty's death. His reply was that "Some had it and some don't." Being of Scots-Irish heritage, he was mindful of his spending. Some accused him of buying cheaper coffee at Burger King, pouring it into a McDonald's cup and enjoying breakfast with his buddies at McDonald's. He enjoyed the suppers prepared, free of charge, by Zion Church.

Occasionally, Lake would phone on a Sunday afternoon, after his nap, and invite me to ride with him to Walmart in Lancaster. He bought his groceries and we shared stories of our McCain families. He told me he would like to take enough piano lessons to play just one hymn for church. How surprised he felt the congregation would be. How sorry I am we never got to learn a hymn. At his funeral I learned Karen, his daughter, took piano lessons from Mrs. Sarah Walker. Mrs. Walker was my piano teacher as well. When Karen practiced, Lake would always ask her to play "Rain Drops Falling on Your Head." Just before the Recessional, the organist played a few lines of this song. I so loved that expression of love and remembrance. Karen told me it helped to keep her from being so sad about her daddy's death. Recently Karen told me a wonderful story about her daddy and her grandfather Kirk McCain. When Lake came home from work, she and her father would often go to Aunt Myrtle's to check the garden. Uncle Kirk would open the screen door and call for her to run in the house so he could give her a Big Hug! Karen followed her father almost everywhere.

It is April 26, 2015. I have found some dates I want to record about Aunt Myrtle and Uncle Kirk's family.

<u>Child number one:</u> **Mildred Kirk McCain** was born March 1, 1919, married on April 2, 1953 to Ross C. Hinson, born December 2, 1911. There children were as follows:

James Richard Hinson, born January 1, 1945, married on June 27, 1971 to Anne Morris, born January 17, 1947.

Ronald Kirk Hinson, born December 31, 1950, died January 2, 1951.

Twins Eugenia Kay Hinson and Rachel Ann Hinson born November 19, 1954.

Only Eugenia (Jeannie) survived.

<u>Child number two:</u> **Robert Dale McCain**, born April 1, 1923, married on February 23, 1948 to Margie Glenn McCain, born February 22, 1929. To them were born:

Glenn Dale McCain, born March 12, 1949, married January 28, 1968 to Marcie Couick, born May 2, 1948. Their son was

Mark Glenn McCain, born June 22, 1970

Douglas Kirk McCain, born January 20, 1956, married on February 16, 1991 to Janice Gregory, born July 10, 1957.

Rosemary Ann McCain, born February 27, 1961

Michael Paul McCain, born April 27, 1968

<u>Child number three:</u> **Harry Lake McCain,** born July 11, 1926, married on February 28, 1952 to Betty Jean Lane, born April 9, 1933. Their children were Roger and Karen.

1. Roger Lake McCain, born March 1, 1953, married May 27, 1972 to Susan Hogan, born March 28, 1954. To them were born: Shawn Lewis McCain, born July 9, 1976, and Joshua Kirk McCain, born May 6, 1979.

Roger married October 25, 1986 to Pam Putman, born September 13, 1960

Their daughter is Morgan Rae McCain, born November 14, 1987

Roger married July 28, 1992 to Judy Everett. Their daughter is Addis, born April 7, 1952. Her daughter, Leah Addis, was born December 1978.

2. Karen Lane McCain Baxley b. June 29, 1957, married Don William Baxley Dec. 5, 1987. He was born April 1, 1959. Karen and Don have two daughters: Chandler Lane Baxley b. Mar. 20, 1990, and Bailey Elizabeth Baxley b. July 17, 1993. Chandler married Donald Richard Kirkley on April 11, 2015. He was born Nov. 20, 1990.

<u>Child number four:</u> **Joe Ewart McCain**, born June 19, 1929, died Oct. 3, 2013, married on Oct. 28, 1954, Betty Mullins who was born August 22, 1931. To them were born: two boys:

Connie Lee McCain 1903-1990 and Sadie Carter McClain 1908-1962

Connie and Sadie's Family: Jo Nell, Bob, Beverly, David, Pam
with children

Connie's daughter Mary Starnes and
husband Drake Starnes

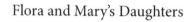

Flora and Mary's Daughters

Family
members
of brothers
Sam and
Connie
McCain

1. John Mullins McCain, born January 27, 1961, married August 17, 1985, Rhonda Joy McAteer, born May 26, 1960. To them were born:

Lauren Elizabeth McCain, born January 24, 1989

Katelin Ashley McCain, born January 1, 1994

2. Joseph Henry McCain, born July 6, 1963, married Patricia Khoury born April 22, 1964. They were married June 3, 1987.

Their children are Alexandria Mullins McCain, born August 30, 1994, and Hannah Nichole McCain, born July 1, 1996

It saddens me to report, there are only four grandchildren of Lizzie and Bob McCain at this writing: Gladys Elizabeth McCain Kerr, Robert Maxwell McCain, Jr., Robert Lee McCain, and Emma Lynn McCain Twitty.

Connie McCain Family

Below is a short autobiographical sketch written by Connie McCain's son Robert Lee McCain that tells the story of his father and their family.

Robert Lee and Jo Nell Starnes McCain

Bob and Jo Nell are both natives of Union County and are retired from the Union County School System. Bob was a teacher and principal, and Jo Nell was a teacher and elementary supervisor. Bob earned his Associate of Science Degree from Presbyterian Junior College in 1954 and his Bachelor of Science Degree from Davidson College in 1956. He earned both his Masters (1965) and an Advanced Certificate in Administration and Supervision (1975) from UNC Chapel Hill.

Bob's career has included eight years as a teacher in the Union County School System, two years of military service at Fort Jackson and Fort Bragg, nine years as an elementary school principal, and eleven years as a middle school principal. He also worked in real estate sales for six years and taught at South Piedmont Community College for two years. Bob is a member of Walkersville Presbyterian Church where he has served as an elder, clerk of the session, Sunday school teacher, and trustee. He enjoys collecting coins and antiques, metal detecting, hunting, and fishing.

Robert Lee McCain, Nina's first cousin, was born December 1, 1933. He married Jo Nell Starnes on June 9, 1957. Jo Nell was born May 23, 1934. Their children are Michael Robert McCain, born April 9, 1961. Mike died September 28, 1982. Beverly Anne McCain Haney was born March 21, 1962. Beverly married Dean Edmund Haney on August 18, 1984. Dean was born May 18, 1960. Their children are Lauren Elizabeth Haney, born May 30, 1988 and Meredith Brenda Haney, born January 31, 1993. David Lee McCain was born April 17, 1966. David married Pamela Rose Winders on September 24, 1989. Pam was born December 13, 1966. They have one daughter, Sarah Katherine McCain, born October 9, 1992.

McCain, This Sunday, August 31, 2014, was a "Visit My Cousins Day." Bob and Jo Nell have been helping me with names and dates for Uncle Connie's family. Rosemary McCain, Dale's daughter, allowed me to borrow a photo album to copy pictures. Here is a story about Aunt Sadie and Maxwell's children. Remember school started in July, way back when, and recessed for several weeks to pick cotton. Cousin Bob remembers that my Daddy wanted the three of us -Gladys, Robert, and Carole- to learn the meaning of "WORK." We were sent to Aunt Sadie's to stay several days and we were to pick cotton. Dear Aunt Sadie made the three of us sacks in which to pick our cotton. I bet they were little cloth sugar sacks! The story goes that Gladys picked pretty well, Robert just stood and stared, and Carole cried!

Bob and I enjoyed thinking about holidays at Granny Lizzie's house. He remembered my Mama always brought the turkey. He wondered where she got that big bird! The men always went bird hunting on Thanksgiving Day. Bob said if the hunt did not go well, the men just tossed ears of corn into the tree limbs and took shots at the corn.

Uncle Connie and Aunt Sadie's Children

1. **Mary Elizabeth McCain** (Born) November 24, 1927 (Died) June 17, 1986
Married Thomas Drake Starnes on December 9, 1944 (Born) November 22, 1924 (Died) July 29, 2001. Three children were born to this marriage:
a. Nancy Lucille Starnes (Born)June 12, 1946: Married Danny Killian October 3, 1970
b. Thomas Samuel Starnes (Born) September 27, 1947: Married Jane B. Winchester February 17, 1967
c. Barbara Jean Starnes (Born) May 1, 1959: Married Dennis Bowers June 20, 1980: Married Gary Medlin August 16, 2003
2. **Flora Yvonne McCain** (Born) July 22, 1931 (Died) September 21, 1962
Married Joe Ware Gordon: October __, 1952 (Born) August 24, 1927 (Died) April 25, 1970
Three children were born to this marriage:
a. Debra Jean Gordon (Born) October 4, 1953: Married Dennis Oren Robinson August 21, 1976
b. Sharon Delores Gordon (Born) February 3, 1955: Married Richard Bennett Simpson April 2, 1977
c. Mitchell Joe Gordon (Born) September 21, 1962: Married Pamela Glennie Norwood May 21, 1983
3. *Robert Lee McCain* (Born) December 1, 1933

Married Jo Nell Starnes June 9, 1957 (Born) May 23, 1934

Three children were born to this marriage:

a Michael Robert McCain (Born) April 9, 1961 (Died) September 28, 1982

b. Beverly Anne McCain (Born) March 21, 1962) Married Dean Edmund Haney (Born) May 18, 1960

c. David Lee McCain (Born) April 17, 1966: Married Pamela Rose Winders on September 24, 1989 (Born) December 13, 1966

Robert Maxwell McCain Family

Below is a letter I wrote to our former neighbors Judy and Brian Tenny on December 28, 2012, regarding our house on the corner of Brevard and King Streets. This will tell you a great deal about my parents and siblings.

The House on the Corner of Brevard and King Streets

My parents, Isa Gladys Winslow and Robert Maxwell McCain Sr., were married in this house on Wednesday night, November 23, 1932. Mama and several other teachers at Waxhaw School including Martha Rone, Lois Womble, and Ruth Holshouser boarded with the homeowners Geneva Walkup Rone and her husband Sam. Mr. Sam "ran" the drugstore downtown on the corner of Broad and North Main Streets. Martha Rone was "Mr. Sam's" niece. Lois played the piano for the ceremony. Mama borrowed Mrs. Willie Broome's piano. She lived across the street. Ruth was the soloist and sang "The Sweetest Story Ever Told." The Reverend Garth was the minister. None of Mama's family could come from Belvidere, NC, but Granny Lizzie McCain was there. Mr. Jim Steele constructed a lovely arch, painted white, under which the bride and groom stood. There were two wooden stands and two white wicker baskets filled with flowers. The house was small and Mama said with the other girls all trying to get dressed, she was the last in line. How beautiful she was in a blue velveteen, long evening gown. Daddy was quite handsome in his new blue surge suit. Usually he wore a bow tie. After the ceremony, the happy couple drove the McCain family car to Charlotte to spend their honeymoon night at the Hotel Charlotte. Thursday, November 24th was Thanksgiving Day, and they were invited to Daddy's niece's home for lunch.

Mama and Daddy had already rented the house on the corner of Brevard and South Providence Streets. Mama just walked across the street to teach second grade. Daddy walked downtown to his job at Farmers' Ginning and Trading Company. He worked on Friday and Saturday and Mama returned to her classroom on Monday. In those days, School Boards frowned on lady teachers being married. Mama had worn her engagement ring on a chain around her neck before the wedding, hoping to protect her job. Nevertheless, she was fired the following year, and Frances Davis took her place. "Frankie" was second grade teacher for

Robert Maxwell McCain and wife Isa Gladys Winslow McCain
1900-1984   1903-1993

me, my brother Robert Maxwell McCain, Jr., and my sister, Lelia Carole McCain Lewis. All three of us were born at home in our parents first home. When I was six, we moved across the road to Luke and Lottie Gamble's house in the middle of King Street. That house was built by Mr. Weir. I lived there until I was married to James Donald Kerr on July 28, 1961.

My four years of undergraduate college (1952-1956) were spent in Red springs, NC, at Flora Macdonald College. Later, I was in graduate school at Peabody College in Nashville, Tennessee (1956-57). With my MA degree in mathematics education, I was off to my first teaching position at Williamsburg Junior High School, Arlington, Virginia. My second year in Virginia, I was tapped to teach accelerated mathematics classes. My dear friend, Delores (Dolly) Kirkpatrick Carroll was in two of my classes. We are grateful for a lasting and renewed friendship which has been ongoing since 2000. After three years in Arlington, I accepted a mathematics-music position at Horace Mann Junior High School in San Diego, California. In June, 1961, I returned to Waxhaw, North Carolina, to be married. My only son, James Maxwell Kerr, was born December 1, 1966. For thirty-eight years I taught mathematics, full-time, at Wingate College, now Wingate University. Since 1999, I have worked as a private piano teacher and worked part-time at Wingate University until January 2011. I continue to substitute for Union County Public Schools and Union Academy, our charter school. My only grandson, Williams McCain Kerr, is an honor student at Union Academy. This year he is in tenth grade and is taking pre-calculus and honors courses. James married Dana Michelle Atchley on May 20, 1995. I had just had rotator cuff surgery and had a sling on my right arm. My dream to visit Scotland came to pass in 2000, after Achilles tendon surgery. I flew to Ireland with a boot on my right foot!

My home since the winter of 1987 has been at 6629 Raymond Helms Road, Waxhaw, North Carolina. I built a home on Daddy's cotton farm. Waxhaw is only ten minutes away and I am happy and quite at peace. The Waxhaw Woman's Club asked me to write their One Hundred Years of History. The book *Crossing the Street* was completed in the spring of 2011. Please get a copy. You may enjoy the journey!

My Childhood Home, 409 King Street, Waxhaw, NC

On Sunday, July 22, 1934, I was born just across the street from the Waxhaw School. This was the home my parents rented since 1932. When I was six or seven years old, my daddy and my mother purchased our home on King Street from the Waxhaw Bank and Trust Co. I believe the year was 1941, and I believe the purchase price was $500. My brother Robert was almost four, and Carole was a new baby.

Before the McCains moved in, the house was occupied by a Dr. and Mrs. Whims and later by Luke and Lottie Walkup Gamble. The Gambles had two daughters, Nancy and Lucia. Lucia was my first playmate. We loved that big front porch with the brick banister, and we played house in the basement. We loved the chicken house and the barn in the back yard. The garage had lots of old items we could use in our pretending adventures. Before the Gambles and Whims, I believe the Weirs lived there and perhaps built the house. On the morning of June 23, 2014, I awakened thinking about the trap door under the stairs which led to the basement. It was an adventure to go slowly down the steps into the darkness when I was young. As I aged, I was truly afraid to use those steps into the basement. Mama used to can beans, tomatoes, soup mixture, fig preserves, pears, and maybe apples. She kept jars, filled with yummy food for the winter, along with empty jars on the dirt shelves of the basement. Some story, right!

Mrs. Cora Lee Guion and her sister, Julia Howard, lived on one side and Campbell and Lucille Myers lived on the other. Mrs. Guion was a widow whose husband was a physician. Her son, Howard, fought in World War II. I remember writing to him. The Myers had two daughters and two sons. The boys were very "mean" to me. Down the street on the corner lived Dr. and Mrs. Burgess. They were grandparents to the Eargle children. Granny Burgess baked tea cakes for me. Dr. Burgess was editor of *The Waxhaw Enterprise*. He raised goats and drank the milk. Yuk!

Mama and Daddy got married in the house on the upper corner (Brevard and King). Mrs. Geneva Rone lived there. Mama and several other school teachers boarded with her. Across the street from them lived Mr. and Mrs. R. J. Belk. Mr. Belk ate cabbage every day. He operated the Belk Department Store in Waxhaw. Down the street were the Luther Bakers, Mrs. Metta Nisbet (my first piano teacher), and Mr. and Mrs. George McCain. Cousin George had a cow and some pigs. His daughter Madeline kept an alligator in a pond in the front yard when she came to visit. Their daughter, Ruth, was my third grade teacher. To earn a little money for candy at The Farmers' Store, I picked up acorns in a syrup bucket and sold them to Cousin George for a nickel. Another neighbor was Willie Broome. Mama borrowed Mrs. Broome's piano, moved it across to Geneva Rone's house, and her friend, Lois Whomble (Abernathy) played this piano for Mama and Daddy's wedding. Ruth Holshouser (Barnhardt) was the soloist, and she sang, "The Sweetest Story Ever Told." Bill Sensenbrenner sang this same song for Mama and Daddy's 50th Anniversary Party.

When I began piano with Mrs. Metta, we had no piano at my house. I practiced in Granny Burgess's living room, which was never heated in the winter. I had to play with my gloves on. Daddy saw that I got a piano before the next winter! I think that upright Steinway is still at Carole's house. I have Gray Austin, attorney, researching the builder and the date that our house was built.

Alex Sims, son of Will Sims, told Ann Price this story: Will Sims was retiring from the Farmers' Store in Waxhaw. He recommended Connie McCain, my Daddy's brother, to take his place at the store. Before he could finalize this suggestion, my Daddy, Robert Maxwell McCain, came into the store to apply for the job. He got the job and worked faithfully until he was 73 years old. He was 26 when he started to work at the Farmers' Store. He operated the cotton gin, served as cotton buyer, and became manager and treasurer. What a model businessman he was. He allowed farmers to buy seed and fertilizer on credit in the spring. When the cotton was ginned in the fall, they would "settle up." Ladies in Waxhaw would telephone their grocery orders, and Daddy always had a delivery boy to walk or drive them to their residences. Bills were to be paid at the end of the

With son
James Maxwell
Kerr Easter 2015

Gladys Elizabeth McCain Kerr

1941

Donald, James and Gladys Kerr

1953 Freshman Flora Macdonald
College

Gladys at the Ancestral Home of Andrew Jackson in Antrim, Northern Ireland

(L) Gladys McCain age 3 with friend Lucia Gamble

Aunt Charlotte, Mama's "Help"

Mother, sister Carole, Gladys, Daddy, brother Robert, Jr.

Sister Carole Lewis in New York City 2010. At right is tatted bookmark by our mother Isa McCain

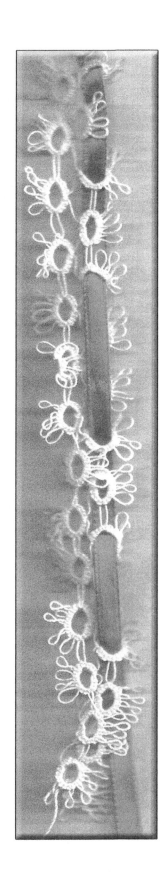

Gladys Kerr at DAC project dedication and dressed in McCain tartan purchased during visit to County Antrim, Scotland 2000

James Kerr and Wife Dana Atchley Kerr

Gladys Kerr Family: Gladys (Nina), Son James Kerr and His Wife Dana

McCain Kerr

(L-R) Brooke McLaughlin, Brenda Atchley, Catherine Holmes, Dana Kerr, Gladys Kerr

James Kerr

James Kerr as young man

Williams McCain Kerr
Age 6 with his puppy

Williams McCain Kerr, son of James
Senior Year High School

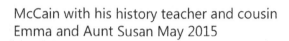

McCain with his history teacher and cousin Emma and Aunt Susan May 2015

McCain with Grandmother Kerr

McCair Kerr and Judy Kennedy

McCain and his father James in Venice

month.   In 2010 the store became a new restaurant after having been the Bridge and Rail Restaurant for over 25 years. John and Terry named this new business: Maxwell's Tavern!

In 2014, the celebration of Waxhaw's 125th anniversary, I was invited to locate myself in front of The Farmers' Store to tell stories about my Daddy and the store. On July 4, 2014, James, McCain, and I were invited to ride on the Waxhaw Business Association Float: Theme: "Heritage and Family" or "Past and Future." In 1989, I was Chairperson of the Centennial Celebration Committee. The Fourth of July Parade was initiated and has been ongoing each year since. That makes me very happy.

Twice Told Tales: Other Memories of My Childhood and Education

I was the first child, born on a hot Sunday morning, July 22, 1934, around 10:00 am, and I weighed in at about 8 pounds 3 ounces. Dr. Whims from across the street was Mama's doctor. She was expecting to have a hard time, so Dr. Whims called in Dr. George Smith from Monroe. Aunt Lessie, Mama's sister, and her daughter, Lelia Lee, came to be with Mama and Daddy.   If Mama died, Aunt Lessie was to take me to Grandma Winslow in Belvidere, NC. I think my Daddy would never have let that happen. Mama lived to have two more children, Robert Maxwell, Jr., born January 7, 1937, weighing 7 pounds, and Lelia Carole, born December 6, 1940, completely bald and weighed 9 pounds. Mama said each time she opened her eyes, Daddy was looking at me in my little green bed, which I still have. Robert had a bassinet which my grandson McCain used. Robert and Carole both slept in the little green bed.

Daddy always had some "help" for Mama. I well remember Aunt Charlotte, Aunt Hannah, Mabel Robinson and her sister Willie Pearl. I heard Mama say the young girls were paid 25 cents a day! I was so jealous of Robert. I had to have a bottle when he had one, and I pinched his little hands. I was willful and stubborn. Once I ran down the hall with Mama's prize sugar bowl, and she ran after me. I threw it down and, of course, it broke. Once Mama broke her arm hurrying out into the yard when I came home crying. Dr. Payne was called to the house. Daddy was helping the doctor pull the arm back into place, and naturally I was right there in the way. The doctor ordered me out of the room.

While I was still demanding a bottle, at almost three years of age, I loved to ride with Daddy to Monroe when he went on business. I had my bottle. When we got home, I asked for the bottle and Mama told me we left it in Monroe. I never asked for that bottle again!

My first playmate was Lucia Gamble who lived in the house across the street. When I was about six, Daddy bought Lucia's house, and that was my home until I married in July, 1961. Lucia would make peanut butter crackers and chocolate milk, which we shared on the steps of the Kings Street Baptist Church. Lucia, her sister Nancy, some cousins, and I would put on plays and invite our parents to attend. One day those naughty girls rolled me up in a rug. They tormented me by telling me I had "ancestors."

Before I was six, I would run over to the school yard, just across from our house, and play with the children at recess. Bill Henry was the custodian and he was my buddy. He ate his breakfast in the boiler room each day, and he brought me an egg biscuit. The old two-story brick school was home for my first grade. My teacher was Mrs. Eulalia Byrum. I so loved her and loved school. One day she invited me to go home with her for the afternoon. That winter our school building burned; it seemed the boys in shop class had been working on an old car and the fire started in that area. The fire was so intense, we feared our house might burn. For the balance of the year, I went to school in the basement of our Presbyterian Church. The cafeteria was in the Woman's Club Building. We passed by Collins Thompson's Store as we walked from one location to another. One day I asked for ice cream, telling Mr. Thompson my Daddy would pay him. Some fifty or sixty years later, I remembered to pay Mr. Thompson. I recited a poem in my first chapel program. It was titled: "Have You Seen My Doggie?" When the principal, Mr. Kenneth Miller, introduced me, he told the audience I had been coming to school all my life. Our lovely new brick school was ready for me to enter second grade. That was a rush job of construction! Another tragedy happened about that time. Robert was five years old and was at the store with Daddy while Mama was next door getting a permanent. Bill Austin was across the road changing a tire, and Robert started walking across the road to watch. He was struck by a car, driven by a lady who stopped and was quite concerned. Mama and Daddy took him immediately to the hospital. Mama still had all the curlers attached to her head. Thank our Good Lord, he had only a cut on his ear and was bumped and bruised badly...no serious injury.

Can you believe I was allowed to go home for lunch the entire time I was a student at Waxhaw Elementary and Waxhaw High School? If it rained or snowed, I was given money to eat in the lunch room, operated by Mrs. Margaret Kell, a really good cook. One day I was so excited to get to ride the school bus with Patricia Taylor, one of my classmates.

Mrs. Frances (Frankie) Thompson was my second grade teacher. She was as nice and kind as Mrs. Byrum. She read us wonderful stories such as "The Little Match Girl" and stories about princesses and princes. She taught us to do the dance, the Minuet. We had the most outstanding chapel programs. We had a Womanless Wedding. We had Talent Shows. That year I had pneumonia and missed a lot of school. My classmate, Iris Cockrell Davis, reminded me the entire second grade came to my home to visit while I was so ill. I got a terrible cold from walking with Mama to deliver Robert's birthday invitations. The only available medicine was sulphur drug. How I loved being in our Operettas. After I finished college and became a teacher, Frankie and I became the dearest friends. What glorious times we shared working for the town of Waxhaw on the outdoor drama *Listen and Remember*, the Centennial Celebration for Waxhaw, and the Fourth of July Parade. These are still ongoing town events! Frankie sponsored me for *Delta Kappa Gamma*, the Honorary Teachers' Society. She lived to meet and love my grandson McCain. She always had a Christmas gift for him. Camp Meeting was ever so special to Frankie and Collins, for they always had all their nieces and nephews staying over. I was welcome at their tent. Sitting on the porch and watching people was a favorite past-time.

When I was about seven or eight, Mama had the three of us on the train going to Belvidere. There were soldiers on the train. One of the soldiers either put a snake on the train or he noticed one was on the train, and he caught it. We three McCain kids just kept right on eating our picnic lunch. Mama was pretty nervous about the snake.

When I was eight years old and in third grade, I felt so grown up. I was taking piano lessons from Mrs. Metta Nisbet, who lived four houses down my street. Her recitals were in her home, and she always served pound cake and ice cream! Miss Ruth McCain was my third grade teacher, and she was a distant cousin. I loved learning to multiply, and I could read much better. Practicing my piano at Dr. Burgess's house was hard because when winter came the room was cold. My dear Daddy saw to it Santa brought me an upright Steinway piano for my very own. After I was married and teaching piano lessons myself, I bought a Baldwin console, which I continue to teach lessons on today. I never did learn to spell very well, but I was determined, at this age to be number one in my class. I did not mind doing homework and practicing piano. Family, church, and school consumed my life.

Fourth grade was a joy! I had Miss Mary Knox for my teacher. She had red, curly hair and was a young lady. She boarded with Mary Lee Nesbit. Mama invited her to have supper with us and we enjoyed visiting on our front porch. I remember she asked me not to ever smoke! Soon after leaving Waxhaw, Miss Knox married Harry Laurie. He has died, but Mary is still living. Her sister, Betty, married Judson Joyner. I saw Betty and Judson at the Waxhaw Presbyterian Church recently. She told me Mary continues to come visit her. How I wish I could see her once more. Geography and North Carolina history were new subjects in fourth grade. History is one of my favorites, along with math!

Mrs. Lois Collins Sims taught fifth grade. At Waxhaw we had only one section of each grade level. Fractions and decimals fascinated me. Mrs. Sims challenged me to reach for the best I could do. Beginning in the fifth grade and on through the twelfth grade I never missed a day of school! I bet I went to school sick many a day. I continued to claim a front seat because I had trouble seeing the blackboard. Mrs. Sims was a close friend of Frankie Thompson and they worked together on special events. One day some students were talking and not paying attention. Mrs. Sims turned around and gave this ultimatum: every student in this class is to write 500 times "I must not talk in class." The assignment was due in the next day. I was not talking; usually I was well behaved in school. I so resented having to write all those lines, and I vowed when I began teaching to never punish the entire class for the bad behavior of a few. I kept in touch with Mrs. Sims until she died. We attended the Presbyterian Church in Waxhaw, and we both belonged to the Waxhaw Woman's Club.

A stern old maid, Miss Clara Purser was my sixth grade teacher. We laughed when she would pull on her girdle! She was smart and expected us to spend time and energy on our assignments. She was dating Jesse Williams, the Waxhaw banker. She would ride with him in his automobile, sitting very close to the driver! I always enjoyed reading, so history and geography were again exciting. I tolerated science, but math remained my favorite. My boyfriend was Olin Byrum, nephew of my first grade teacher. He had curly hair and was quite handsome! That year when I was twelve, I joined the Waxhaw Presbyterian Church. Meeting with the session was frightening to me. I had at six recited the Child's Catechism, and this year I recited the Shorter Catechism. Mama helped me learn a page each day after school, sitting on our front porch. Oh, how my Daddy loved that front porch!

I was continuing to take piano from Mrs. Sarah Chapman Walker. A recital was on the horizon, and I was trying to play soft ball at school. My thumb got in the way of the ball, and I was in great pain. I performed regardless, but not too well. We piano students usually took two lessons a week, for $5.00 a month, imagine! I walked to Mrs. Walker's home either on Monday and Thursday or Tuesday and Friday. I was supposed to practice one hour each day! Mrs. Laura Howey, wife of our local dentist, whose office was upstairs over the bank, was my teacher. She was tall, wore old lady shoes, subdued colors in her dresses, rarely smiled, used composition books with stitched binding for her ancient notes, but she was a competent, fair teacher. She was a "No Nonsense" lady. I was truly blessed, having grown up in a small town, to have had for the most part, excellent teachers.

In eight grade I had Mrs. Ida Rodman, a Colonial Dame, and this dear lady gave me the most elegant luncheon when I was about to become a bride! She gave me a sterling silver ice bucket with tongs! I have already given this precious gift to my daughter-in-law, Dana. Mrs. Ida was a member of the Waxhaw Presbyterian Church, so I saw her on Sundays. She was so smart, not pretty at all, a little heavy, and very nervous. She continually pushed her hair away from her face. I learned how to diagram sentences, to define parts of speech, lots of math and history, sadly again, I did not care for science. I am trying hard to remember if Mr. Arthur Newkirk also shared teaching eight grade. I had moved from the elementary side of the school building to the high school wing. I do remember two classmates, Cletus and Margaret got into a real fight over a boy, and he (Newkirk) went into the hallway to "break it up." In July of 2014, I read in the newspaper, a teacher, Arthur Newkirk, Jr., was to be recognized for excellent coaching and teaching. Could this be a son of my eighth grade teacher? Mrs. Rodman wanted the class to have a hayride and picnic at Massey's pond (Esther's Daddy's farm).

Neither Esther nor I were allowed to go; our parents feared serious misconduct. And indeed some boys and girls did what teenagers are inclined to do, my, my. The next day at school, Mrs. Rodman cried and tried desperately to explain the infraction and reflection it left on her. I suppose I was then glad I did not go. A really good memory is the Train Trip to Atlanta with Mrs. Walker and about twenty students! We stayed in the Piedmont Hotel, after being carefully taught how to conduct ourselves in the hotel and at restaurants. Billy Parks Davis, throwing caution to the wind, ordered three different kinds of potatoes one day! We heard the New York Philharmonic Orchestra, went to Stone Mountain, and enjoyed museums and art.

Soon I was in high school. I will try to name the entire faculty (remember when I was a senior, there were only 23 students to graduate). They were Mr. Tedder, agriculture; Mrs. Nickolson, Miss White and Miss Margaret Crosby, home economics; Nelly Shannon, Polly Boger, Mr. Kale, and Mr. Young, social science; Mr. Hamilton, coach and science; Mrs. Crenshaw and Mr. Lathan, mathematics; Joanne Matthews and Mr. Lathan, French; Mrs. Sarah

Walker, piano and glee club; Miss Gladys Craven, commercial; and Mrs. Margaret Kell, dietitian. Howard Lathan was a Union County Commissioner and often had meetings in Monroe; those days I was teacher! He would leave us every now and then to go to the boiler room for a smoke! Mr. Kale and Mr. Young were my principals, and they taught social science. They, too, had to miss class, and I was sometimes in charge. When testing, once in a while, some of my friends tried to cheat off my paper, but I just covered my answers because I wanted to be number one in my class! I only had the opportunity to take Algebra I, Algebra II, and Geometry. How did I ever major in mathematics?

I think I was accompanist for the Glee Club all four years. My Junior Year, I was really busy: Class President (which meant I had to plan our Junior-Senior Banquet), President of the Glee Club, Secretary of the Beta Club, Member of the Wahico Annual Staff, and Secretary of the Bible Club. Our Junior Year, Mr. Kale, principal, took the Beta Club to Myrtle Beach. It was my first time to see the ocean!

Senior, at last. My class was the first to make a trip to Washington, D. C., after a long dry spell! How exciting for me to see all the history I had studied for all these years. We had fun as well, dropping water balloons from the windows in our hotel, enjoying all the rides at Glen Echo Park, and experiencing new foods. During 1951-1952, I was Class Treasurer, Class Historian, a member of Future Homemakers, the Glee Club, Editor of Wahico, President of the Beta Club, and a CHEERLEADER! Our sports were confined to baseball and basketball, but we were indeed proud of our teams, girls and boys.

James C. Davis took me to the Junior-Senior Banquet my Junior Year. It was held at the Monroe Hotel, and I was class president and totally responsible for the planning. I thought it was super wonderful. I played piano for Sue Gamble to sing "Somewhere over the Rainbow", which was the theme for our event. Our Senior Year, I went with Don Kerr to the Junior-Senior Banquet, at the Waxhaw Woman's Club. It was nothing to brag about! Each time, I had a lovely corsage. I believe I wore my pink taffeta recital dress in the eleventh grade, and Aunt Ruth made me a gorgeous white silk with ruffles all down the skirt for my twelfth grade banquet. How very proud I was to be Class Valedictorian. I worked and worked on my speech. Then in my excitement, I left my trophy on the stage when it was time for the recessional. Another outstanding honor for me was to receive Mrs. Walker's medal for Making the Most Progress that year. This happened two times for me, and she engraved on the back of the first medal, Second Time. Mrs. Walker took us on a bus to Gastonia for Piano Competition every year. Making a score of Superior was a tough job.. You played two selections: one that was required and one of your own selection. What good experience and training for us. My junior year I gave a recital all by myself. I even played one movement from a Mozart *Concerto*. Over and over Mrs. Walker said, "You may be the only one who can play." I took this remark seriously when I was a freshman at Flora Macdonald College, and I arranged my schedule to major in mathematics and minor in music! I also got a teaching minor in history and science; imagine that! The scholarship I got and my working scholarships-- serving tables in the dining hall, taking meals to the

The Farmers' Store in Waxhaw, NC

Robert Maxwell McCain (L) with Will Davis and Jesse Williams

Maxwell McCain's Home in Waxhaw and birth place of their three children
Gladys, Robert and Carole

Robert Maxwell McCain, Sr. (b. 1900) Robert McCain, Jr. (b. 1937) and wife Sarah Drake Dodd

Robert McCain's sons Trent (front), Mid, Gib, and Rob

Robert Maxwell McCain, Jr. Family

The Wedding of Laura and Mid McCain 1992. (L-R) Gladys McCain Kerr, Grandmother Isa Gladys McCain, father Robert, Laura, Mid, Carole, Craig, and Andy

Gib with his daughter Morgan Hailey McCain born August 20, 1998

Robert and Drake's Grandsons: Robert Maxwell, IV, and Scott
(Children of Rob and Connie)

Gib and Jen McCain's children: (L) Matthew, David, Morgan, and Max

Mid McCain Family: Mid, Laura, Logan, Emery, and Stewart

Mid's Son Logan 2015 Prom

Trent McCain's Children: Taylor, Win

Robert McCain's Grandchildren Win and Taylor, son and daughter of Drs. Trent and Darla McCain. Both children will be attending ballet schools during the 2015 summer. Taylor at Harid Conservatory Ballet School in Boca Rotan, Florida, and the American Ballet School in Los Angeles and Win at Ballet West Academy/the University of Utah.

Dana's brother Brett and children

Scott and Robert McCain

Mary Sheldon and
Bradie Holmes

Taylor and Win
McCain

Lynn and Boyet's Grandson
Bristol

Lynn and Boyet Twitty's
Grandsons

infirmary, tutoring math students, serving the faculty table, and working in the Testing and Planning Office for Roger Decker--- all helped Daddy with my tuition and other expenses.

My freshman year in college I had a terrible roommate, Norma Kelly. I wonder what happened to her. Eventually she was sent home. Pat Farmer Moore roomed next door and took me under wing. She would go with me to my piano exams and hold my hands to keep my fingers warm until my name was called! My sophomore year, I chose Mary McLean from Raeford for my roommate, and that was a REAL PLUS. After all these years, we are dear friends. We lived on Page Hall, and I became close friends, not only with Pat and Mary, but my list now included Frances Shaw Ashford, Mary Archie Brown McNeill, Carolyn Robinson Lineberger, Sallie Anne Munroe Kirven, Anita Williamson Shore, and Kittye Oliver Sowell. Kittye died just after our 50th FMC Class Reunion, but the rest of us try to "Get Together" at the beach in June and in the mountains in October. I was pretty much a "NERD" in college. I joined Epsilon Society, practiced my piano, went to church, spent a lot of time in the library, and studied almost constantly. Once or twice I went to a movie in downtown Red Springs. I did invite Don Kerr to come for our Senior Dance. We actually had a great time. Ruth Guion Coffey invited me to go with her family to the Ice Capades in Raleigh. Pat and Mary took me home with them for the weekend, many times. I rarely got to come home, except for holidays. I was inducted into the Honor Society (*Phi Beta Kappa*) and received a scholarship to pursue a masters degree at George Peabody College (Peabody-Vanderbilt). My senior year I dated David Gibson from Raeford. This was pretty serious for a year or two.

My first teaching job was at Williamsburg Junior High in Arlington, Virginia. I was there for three years, and I worked with accelerated math students. I taught one year in San Diego, California, math and music. Don came at Christmas, stayed two weeks, brought me a diamond, and in June I drove my 1957 Chevy back to Waxhaw. We were married in the Waxhaw Presbyterian Church, July 28, 1961, and I moved to Kerr Farms. Immediately, I went to Wingate College to teach mathematics. I was full time professor until 2000, and then I taught part-time until the end of 2010. Now I substitute in the Union County Public Schools and at Union Academy, our charter school, where my grandson was a student.

Now as I approach age 80, I realize more and more how the two most significant times in my life were the births of my son James Maxwell Kerr on December 1, 1966, and my grandson Williams McCain Kerr, born March 21, 1997. These two splendid young men have been my reason for "Keeping On." God has richly blessed me. Each day I pray I may render some act of kindness, bless someone, a friend or a stranger.

A Postscript: On Saturday, July 19, 2014, by family including James, Dana, and McCain have invited Esther, Pat, Frances, Mary Archie, and me to have brunch at Ballantyne Resort Hotel in Charlotte. Carolyn and Mary had other plans. The occasion is my 80th birthday! I am too excited to function!

Stories and Fables about My Brother, Robert Maxwell McCain, Jr.

I was about 2 1/2 when Robert was born on January 7, 1937. Dr. George Smith delivered the baby and Mrs. Martha Benton was Mama's nurse. How wonderful, Mama and Daddy now had a girl and a boy! The economy was at a low ebb, but we children never felt neglected nor deprived. Knowing that we were wanted and loved steered us through.

Mrs. Benton not only took care of Mama and Robert, she smocked a little dress for me while she was at our house. I was so jealous of the baby boy. When he had a bottle of eagle brand milk, I had to have a bottle of cow's milk! When he was in his precious little, white, wooden bassinet, I would reach in and pinch him. Once Mama was outside for a minute and left me with Robert. I locked the doors and would not let Mama in the house. Of course, Robert was crying, and Mama had to climb in a window to rescue the baby. Little Gladys got yet another spanking for this naughty act! Robert and I helped Daddy some at the store. I never really enjoyed cooking, cleaning, or sewing, but I loved being at the store with Daddy. My jobs were dusting the shelves and tables with a feather duster, sweeping the oiled wooden floors and the sidewalk outside the front door, and decorating the two showcase windows at the front door. Soon Robert and I could fill the drink box. This was a big tin rectangular bin with cold water, but inside were little green bottles of Coke, Ni High Orange and Grape, Cheerwine, Pepsi, Root Beer, and Ginger Ale. Later Daddy got an ice cream box. He only sold ice cream sandwiches and popsicles. To get a cone of ice cream, we walked up the street to Mr. Henry Gamble's Drug Store. The Farmers' Store always had penny candy in a long glass covered counter: Mary Janes, Tootsie Rolls, Peanut Butter Logs, Jaw Breakers, and Bubble Gum. Even before I could walk to the Farmers' Store, Daddy brought me a piece of candy or a stick of Juicy Fruit Gum each night when he came home. He would put it in his shirt pocket which made it easy for me to find when I climbed on his lap.

Robert was assigned the job of loading feed and seed onto customers' trucks and the distasteful job of catching live chickens from the hen house at the back of the store. Once he captured the chicken, he tied the legs with a string, came into the store, got a brown paper bag, put the chicken inside, punched a hole of the head, and the purchase was ready to deliver. He very much disliked this job!

Along came Carole when I was six years old. She was born just before the Waxhaw School burned. Her birthday was December 6, 1940. Carole weighted in at over nine pounds! Dr. Smith was again Mama's doctor, but the nurse in charge was Mrs. Orr. I do believe I was taken to the store that day until the precious bundle arrived. For whatever reason, I seemed really proud to have a baby sister. I loved play-ing games with Robert and Carole, either in the yard, which was rocky with no grass, or under our house, which was high enough to build a giant playhouse.

Later my duties at the store became more exciting, and Robert was old enough to deliver groceries now. Daddy was teaching me to unlock the wooden money drawer located under the check-out counter. Then he taught me to count money: five pennies in a stack, five nickels in a stack, ten dimes in a stack, four quarters in a stack, and two fifty-cent pieces: then the bills: ones, fives, tens, twenties, etc. always face-up in the same direction. When this was mastered, I was allowed to take the deposit to Mr. Jesse Williams or Miss Lola Burgess at the Waxhaw Bank and Trust Company, just two doors down the street. Eventually, I learned to make out the deposit slip. Daddy never taught me the combination to the safe which sat on the floor next to his desk chair. Oh, I loved that chair. It was so high, had a back, and swilled. His desk was slanted, much like a drafting desk, and had a cage about it with a opening for his customers to stand on the outside but be able to see and hear him. What fun for me to put items in the show-case windows, especially at Christmas, Thanksgiving, or Easter. Daddy always allowed farmers to bring fresh vegetables and fruits to sell and sometimes molasses, or honey, and perhaps some jelly or jam.

When Robert, Carole, and I were growing up there was no day care. Baby sitters were neighbors or grandparentd. There were no parks. Like David Barnes and Harvey Clay Nesbit, we used the Farmers' Store for a gym. We played on the feed sacks, we played hop scotch on the street, we threw balls in the back driveway, and on Saturdays, we went to the movie, just down the street from A. W. Heath Co. There was a western each week and a serial segment which went on for a number of weeks. One Saturday Robert went to the movie alone, wearing his baseball cap. It began to get dark and he had not returned to the store. Mama sent met to fetch him. He was sitting on the front seat, with his cap on, and had seen the movie about three times.

He had no concept of the time. I bet his 10 cent popcorn had run out long ago, and he was getting hungry. At that time an adult ticket to the movie was 35 cents and the child's price was 9 cents. Buddy Austin operated the projector. The entire school at Waxhaw was allowed to walk to the movie when the faculty thought it appropriate-such as *Gone With the Wind*. Dora Lee Wiley reminded me that the children sometimes just took a walk to the Waxhaw Cemetery, which was just back of the school. Robert, Carole, and I were allowed to walk home for lunch each day. I loved rainy days when Daddy gave me lunch money, and Mrs. Sam Kell made soup with peanut butter sandwiches.

I was never an athlete, but Robert was great. He could really pitch a baseball, and he was a great basketball player. Robert was always quiet and mannerly. He had lots of friends and he saved his money Daddy paid him for working at the Farmers' Store. His really big purchase, after a ball glove, was a shiny, red bicycle. He actually let me learn to ride a bike on his new one. We all had roller skates with steel wheels, for you see we had to ride on the sidewalks. We just strapped the skates to our shoes, tightened the clamps, and away we went to the King Street Baptist Church, which had a semicircular turn-around.

I cannot remember Carole going with Robert and me to the cotton gin. That was fascinating and scary to me. I loved climbing into the bed of the wagon or truck and letting the big pipe which sucked the cotton into the gins, actually suck my hair up the pipe! There were four gins, boxes with sharp steel teeth, continually running to pull the seed from the cotton and blow the lint into a special compartment where the bale was packed.

It would take about a 1,000 pounds or more of cotton to produce a 500 pound bale, which was wrapped in burlap and tied with steel bands. Then the bales were trucked off to the depot platform for Bun Simpson to tag and sort for shipping on the train. Oh, how sad my family was when someone at the gas station operated by Clyde Ghant, accidently burned our cotton gin when they were burning trash. Remember, we had no efficient fire department. In the year 2015, there is a state of the art facility and operation to prevent fires.

For a short time Robert and Carole took piano lessons, but I was the one who so wanted to play piano. Carole and Robert played in the Waxhaw Band, trombone for Robert and clarinet for Carole. All three of us were in the Beta Club. Carole and I were also cheerleaders, and Carole and Robert played basketball. Robert was determined to be an outstanding student, academically. He was Valedictorian of his Class of 1955, Waxhaw High School. He was nominated for the prestigious Morehead Scholarship at the University of North Carolina Chapel Hill. He was a semi-finalist, and our family was so proud of him. He had no guidance or support at Waxhaw High School. You see we had no Guidance Counselors, and the principal nor the faculty took time to prepare him for his interview. He drove the 1952 green Chevy, which was Mama and Daddy's first car, to downtown Charlotte. All alone he presented himself to the panel of judges. He did his best to answer questions about his plans for college, his future, how much his family could afford to help with his finances, etc. How nervous he must have been! He did not win the Morehead, but he received a scholarship for tuition. He worked at the Carolina Inn as a waiter and this provided his meals. His roommate was Bruce King, a Waxhaw classmate. He studied hard, did well, received his BA degree in 1959, his Masters in Education in 1962, and his Advanced Administration Degree in 1968. Robert did his student teaching in Sanford, NC. His first job teaching was in Jamestown, NC, and Kenneth Miller was district principal. His wife was a great friend and mentor for Robert. He had a room at Mrs. Wright's home. She was a dear lady. While at Chapel Hill he met Sarah Drake Dodd from Monroe, and in 1962 they were married. The wedding was at Central Methodist Church with a lovely reception at the Monroe Country Club. Robert's next position was principal at Mineral Springs School. He was so loved by students, faculty, and parents. Drake and Robert lived in the little red house in the backyard at her parents' home in Monroe. We called the little house "The Shack." As time marched on, Robert was appointed Title One Director and eventually Assistant Superintendent of Union County Schools. Later the Monroe School System merged with Union County and he had a great deal of responsibility. He was in charge of personnel. Truly he should have been our superintendent! Drake and Robert lived in Charlotte for short time and moved back to Monroe. Their first real home was on Rolling Hills Drive, and they were there for more than thirty years. They were blessed with four wonderful sons, Robert Maxwell McCain, III, David Gibson McCain, Bryan Middleton McCain, and Trent Winslow McCain. Now they have eleven grandchildren. When Robert retired from the school system, he wanted no

Lelia Carole McCain
Lewis 1940- 2011
and Lee Craig Lewis, Jr.
Family

Angie, Drayton, Carole, Craig Lewis

Carole

Carole McCain Third Grade

Carole's son Andrew Craig Lewis

Waxhaw High School Marching Band 1955. Carole McCain (Second Row, Second from Right)

Carole McCain Lewis' Family

Andy and Angie Lewis' Wedding Day

Andy

Carole, Ellis, Robert

Andy Lewis and James Kerr with Grandmother McCain

party or reception; he just packed up his desk and went home. Now he works for his brother-in-law, David Dodd (Dee) at Carolina Pest Control. He and Drake have been ever so kind to me. Robert calls almost every day to be sure I am doing fine. Robert was voted Teacher of the Year at Jamestown. He has received numerous awards, but he is low key about any recognition. My quiet, sly, unassuming little brother. How I love him.

On January 19, 2011, our sister, Carole, died from lung cancer. Robert visited her every day while she was at Hospice. It was a sad, hard time for me, and he was always there to advise and comfort. Now, today January 20, 2015, just the two of us left, and we await the time for our grandchildren to go to college.

I am so proud of you, McCain, for your nomination, like Uncle Robert, as a Morehead Scholarship at the University of North Carolina Chapel Hill. We are all proud of him and of you. Fortunately, you had an opportunity to be coached through a mock interview by your parents before they accompanied you to Charlotte for the interview. I understand you were quizzed by two panels, one at 2 pm and one at 3 pm on January 6, 2015. McCain, you are so qualified and such a dedicated student and volunteer. I know God has plans for you we cannot yet imagine. Thank you, Dear Lord, for blessing me with the most wonderful parents, a special brother and sister, and Waxhaw to call my home.

My Sister Lelia Carole McCain Lewis

McCain, I am so grateful you actually know my brother, Robert, and you knew Carole. When we realized how ill she was in 2010, your Dad asked her what was on her Bucket List. Immediately she said she wanted to go to New York City! Carole had never flown in an airplane. She always loved the beach, beach music, dancing, playing cards, her cigarettes, sleeping late, and goofing off with her friends! She loved life and she loved living!

Earlier I told you she was a nine pound plus baby, and Mama used a powdered milk for her, maybe it was called SMA. She was a chubby little girl until she got to high school. Her hair and makeup had to be just right; her clothes had to be fashionable, and indeed she was a very pretty young lady. Being slim was a must! Food was always important to her. Once Mama sent her to the Farmers' Store for strawberries. She got to the sidewalk behind Lucille Davis' house, sat on the sidewalk and ate all the strawberries! After her marriage, Andy's birth, and her move from Winston-Salem to Waxhaw, she began to gain weight again. Her husband, Lee Craig Lewis, Sr., often took the three of us to eat at the Bridge and Rail or Rippington's in Waxhaw. Several time we did a road trip to Tennessee to visit his son, Lee, and family. We also loved a day trip to Blowing

Rock to browse in the shops on Main Street, check out the Mall, and have a great lunch.

After Carole and I moved to Mama and Daddy's farm, we had time to do things together. She joined the Waxhaw Woman's Club, The Waxhaws Chapter of Daughters of the American Colonists, and served as a state chairman for me when I was state regent. We enjoyed walking up and down our paved road, Raymond Helms, which took me about 15 years to get in place. I will never forget the shock I felt when James, Dana, McCain, and I got home from a two week vacation to Europe and discovered Carole had lung cancer. A few months later mold and mildew were discovered in her home, and I insisted she move in with me until the repairs were completed. How I loved having her. For a time she got up at 6:30 am to ride to Monroe to stay with Dana while I taught math at Wingate University. Then she stayed at my house alone during the day for several weeks. Hospice was coming to monitor her health until December, when it seemed she needed to move to the Hospice Home in Monroe. Robert and I tried to visit every day. I spent several nights with her, for there was a little sofa for me. Dana had us both to her house for Christmas Day dinner. Carole was failing then, but I feel she enjoyed that day. I insisted she go to the New Year's Party at Hospice, but she was too sick and tired to participate. I was teaching part-time, trying to write *The History of The Waxhaw Woman's Club*, and teaching piano lessons. She literally held on that last day until I returned from teaching piano. She died peacefully about 5:30 on Don Kerr's birthday, January 19, 2011. I cry now when I remember how much I loved her and miss her so terribly. Not only was she my sister, she was my dearest friend. She listened to my woes, gave me counsel, encouraged me, and loved me.

Here are a few fun stories about Carole: One day she got chewing gum stuck in her hair. Rather than tell Mama, she got the scissors and cut a large wad of hair, giving herself bangs. She and Ed Guion, who lived next door with his grandmother, pushed all Mrs. Kell's flower pots off her porch banister. I do believe a spanking followed. Another day while Ed's grandmother, Cora Lee Guion, was having a bridge party, he and Carole let the air out of the ladies' tires! Loffie Nesbit, Frances Ellen Simpson, June Wilkerson, and Carole got into lots of mischief. June recently told me Lowell Couick drove a car across the Overhead Bridge with children cowering in the floor of the car! The girls put a Ray Charles' recording in the Methodist Church Bell Tower. A glorious noon-time concert was heard all over town! When her two grandchildren, Drayton and Olivia, were small, she loved to baby-sit. Sometimes Craig would go with her. Andy told me he thinks Drayton is a little like his Dad, but Olivia, definitely, is much like Carole.

Just for one year, I taught in San Diego, California. Robert drove with me to help me get settled, and he flew back to Waxhaw. When school was over in June, Mama and Daddy, sent Carole and her college friend, Carolyn, on the train, to drive back home with me. I cannot begin to recount the experiences we encountered over those thousands of miles! I even allowed those girls to drive my car to Disneyland while we were in California! On the way to the train in Charlotte, Daddy had car trouble, and Carole was sure they would miss the train. They walked up to a house, not knowing who lived there, explained their plight to the lady who opened the door, and low and behold she drove the girls to the train station.

There is a great story about Carole's one and only trip to New York. Carole had never flown on an airplane! We were off to New York City--James, Carole, and Gladys. Dana made all the arrangements on her computer: plane tickets, hotel (The Algonquin, 1920's), restaurant reservations, and play tickets. We had a suite at the hotel: a living room (James slept on the sofa), a bedroom, which Carole and Gladys shared, and a bath. We ate breakfast and several other meals here. James ordered a special car to drive us to locations around the city. This helped him with Carole's wheelchair. Carole slept most of the boat trip around the New York Harbor; she loved the horse and carriage ride through Central Park, Rockefeller Center, church at St. Patrick's where we took Communion, lunch at the Plaza Hotel, pizza delivered to our suite. We saw *Lion King* and a comedy. Carole was a real trouper, and I know she loved every minute of the trip. It would never have happened without James and Dana.

OBITUARY: LELIA CAROLE McCAIN LEWIS

Lelia Carole McCain Lewis died on January 19, 2011. She was born December 6, 1940. Carole was born in Waxhaw, North Carolina, attended Waxhaw Elementary School, and graduated from Waxhaw High School in 1959. She held a BS degree in Education from East Carolina College. Her professional career included teaching sixth grade at Brunson Elementary School in Winston-Salem and third and sixth grades at Wesley Chapel Elementary School and East Union Middle School in Union County. Carole was married to Lee Craig Lewis, Jr., who preceded her in death in 2008. Their son, Andrew Craig Lewis and his wife, Angela and children, Drayton and Olivia, live in Waxhaw. Her stepson, Lee Phillip Lewis and his wife, Kristen and four step-grandchildren, Phillip Lee Lewis and wife, Miranda, Spencer and Alexis Lewis reside in Sevierville, Tennessee. She is survived also by a sister, Gladys McCain Kerr of Waxhaw, a brother, Robert Maxwell McCain, Jr. and wife, Drake, of Matthews, and five nephews: Robert Maxwell McCain, III and wife, Connie; David Gibson McCain and wife, Jennifer; James Maxwell Kerr and wife, Dana; Bryan Middleton McCain and wife, Laura;, and Trent Winslow McCain and wife, Darla.

Carole was a member of First Presbyterian Church in Monroe, North Carolina, where she was a member of the Joy Circle and the Ladies Bible Class. Earlier she had assisted with the Youth Club at First Presbyterian. Carole was an Honorary Member of The Waxhaw Woman's Club, a past member of The Monroe Garden Club, and a member of The Waxhaws Chapter, Daughters of The American Colonists. A Memorial Service will be held at First Presbyterian Church on January 22, 2011, at 2 pm. Visitation at First Presbyterian Church, Monroe, NC, prior to the service, 1:00-1:45 pm. Graveside Service at Greenwood Cemetery, Belmont, North Carolina, will be held at a later date and is private. Memorials may be sent to First Presbyterian Church, 302 East Windsor Street, Monroe, North Carolina 28112 OR to Hospice of Union County, 700 West Roosevelt Blvd. Monroe, North Carolina 28110.

Children and Grandchildren of Robert Maxwell McCain, Sr. and Isa Gladys Winslow McCain

Gladys Elizabeth McCain Kerr, born July 22, 1934, married James Donald Kerr, July 28, 1961. They have one son:

James Maxwell Kerr, born December 1, 1966, married Dana Michelle Atchley, May 20, 1995. They have one son:

Williams McCain Kerr, born March 21, 1997

Robert Maxwell McCain, Jr., born January 7, 1937 married Sarah Drake Dodd McCain, December 27, 1962

They have four sons:

1. Robert Maxwell McCain, III, born February 27, 1964
married Constance Elizabeth Vasoll McCain, February 4, 2000
They have two sons: Robert Maxwell McCain, IV, born February 14, 2001
Scott Alden McCain, born January 31, 2003

2. David Gibson McCain, born July 4, 1966
married Jennifer Anita Matthias McCain, June 4, 1994
They have three sons and one daughter:
David Gibson McCain, Jr., born November 30, 1996
Morgan Hailey McCain, born August 20, 1998
Matthew Matthias McCain, born December 28, 2000
Maxwell Madden McCain, born March 7, 2002

3. Bryan Middleton McCain, born April 6, 1969
married Laura Leigh Stewart McCain, November 28, 1992
They have three children: one boy and twin girls
Logan Middleton McCain, born January 22, 1997
Elizabeth Emery McCain, born August 18, 1999
Sarah Stewart McCain, born August 18, 1999

4. Trent Winslow McCain, born February 28, 1971
married Darla Lynne Hatch McCain, June 20, 1998
They have two children: one boy and one girl
Trent Winslow McCain, Jr., born October 5, 1999
Taylor Drake McCain, born March 26, 2001

Lelia Carole McCain Lewis, born December 6, 1940
married Lee Craig Lewis, Jr., June 14,1964
They have one son: Andrew Craig Lewis, born December 6, 1964
who married Angela Mills Lewis, October 22, 1994

Knox Ratchford McCain
1907-1979
and Ruth Mae
Starnes McCain
1913-1998
Family

Gathering of Uncle Knox
and Aunt Ruth's Family

Boyet and Lynn Twitty
with grandsons
Bristol, Brody, and Braylen

The Bastons: Mark, Allison, Bristol,
Brody, and Braylen

Boyet, Lynn, Allison, Todd Twitty

Arnold and Pat McCain's Daughter Kathy Mandeville and Husband

They have one son and one daughter:
Andrew Drayton Lewis, born March 10, 1997
Olivia Caroline Lewis, born November 17, 2000

Deaths in the family. Lee Craig Lewis, Jr. died December 5, 2008, Lelia Carole McCain Lewis died January 19, 2011. (Carole and Craig are buried in Belmont, NC), Robert Maxwell McCain, Sr., died December 22, 1984, Isa Gladys Winslow McCain died February 9, 1993. Daddy and Mama are buried at Lake Memorial Park in Monroe, NC

Sunday, March 1, 2015
To: Williams McCain Kerr
From: Gladys Elizabeth McCain Kerr

McCain, It is cold and rainy today, but in my heart the world is beautiful and the sun is shining. I rejoice that you have been accepted at UNC Chapel Hill, and now you tell me you have been awarded a wonderful scholarship! "God is so Good." Long ago, the Lord answered my prayer for a child...Here came your Dad, my James! Oh, how I love my son! Then I prayed for a wife to love him and share a lifetime with him...He sent your Mom, Dana...How I love her! Next, I prayed for a grandchild to love and cherish. God made you, McCain, no other ever being exactly like you, and how you have blessed our lives. I know our Heavenly Father has a Very Special Plan for you. Your mission is mammoth and challenging. Please always rely on God for strength, wisdom, direction, and purpose. Please find a church in Chapel Hill and get to know the minister. There will be times you will need advice and a friend. I pray for you just the right roommate. My heart is so full of love and faith in you. If I am privileged to be physically present for your Inauguration Ceremony...What a Day That Will Be. Call me often. You know I will always be there for you!
With all my love,
Nina

Knox McCain Family

Uncle Knox and Aunt Ruth: Children and grandchildren
Daughter: **Emma Lynn McCain Twitty:** born May 29, 1946, husband, Boyet Avery Twitty, Jr: born July 29, 1942 : marriage date: November 24, 1968
Children: Daughter: Allison Dione Twitty Batson: born December 10, 1970, husband, Richard Mark Batson: born May 2, 1971: marriage date: June 26, 1993. Allison and Mark's children: Bristol Knox Batson: born January 4, 1998
Brody Mark Batson: born April 4, 2000
Braylen Jack Batson: born November 1, 2002

Son: **Jonathan Todd Twitty:** born June 5, 1973, wife, Debra Parker Twitty: born September 7, 1963: marriage date: December 4, 1999

Debra's son by a previous marriage: D. J. Rushing: born February 1, 1989, wife, Kristen: born May 9, 1986: marriage date: May 26, 2012

Debra's daughter by a previous marriage: Devane Rushing: born July 22, 1985

I need information about William Thompson McCain and Robert Arnold McCain: McCain, it is Saturday before Easter 2015. Lynn McCain Twitty just mailed information about her two brothers, Bill and Arnold, both deceased. I am most grateful, for Aunt Ruth and Uncle Knox's family has been kind and loving to me since I was a child.

Uncle Knox and Aunt Ruth's boys beginning with the eldest:

1. **William Thomas McCain** Born: January 1, 1934 Died: December 3, 2010

   a. Bill's first son: *William Thomas McCain,* Jr.

   Born: January 4, 1960   Not married

   b. Bill's second son: *James Edward McCain*

   Born: November 1, 1961

   Married Sharon Elizabeth Meadows, April 12, 1987: Sharon Meadows McCain was born January 3, 1965. Their children were

   Ashley Nicole (Nikki) born April 25, 1987,

   Brittany Morgan McCain Lindsey born October 3, 1989:

   Brittany married Corey Lindsey

   Brittany and Corey have one daughter:

   Madeline, born June 2012.

   Brittany's second baby is due very soon.

   c. Bill's third son: *Timothy Scott McCain:* divorced

   Scott had two children:

   Matthew McCain born February 18, 1988 and

   Jessica McCain born January 26, 1991

Aunt Ruth and Uncle Knox's second son:

2. **Robert Arnold McCain:** Born March 24, 1935 Died June 3, 1980

Arnold first married Patricia Anne Guy, September 12, 1958

Pat was born July 22, 1940 and died November 11, 2014: We share a birthday!

   a. Lisa Lynn McCain Lowe was born May 8, 1963. Lisa married David Luther Lowe, February 14, 1983. David Lowe was born June 5, 1963 and died February 8, 2013.
   Lisa and David had three children:

   1) Kelly LeAnne Lowe Heatherly, born August 7, 1984
   Kelly married David Matthew Heatherly, March 20, 2011. David Heaterly born June 17, 1987. Kelly and David have one son, Dakota Lee Heatherly, born March 15, 2011

2) Ashley Nicole Lowe, born March 12, 1987
Ashley had two children:
       Mya Nicole Lowe, born December 10, 2007
       Isiah James Bush, born December 21, 2010
   3) Brandan David Lowe, born February 25, 1991: not married
Arnold's second wife was Alice Street, born December 7, 1942 and died October 8, 1997
Arnold and Alice had two children:
  1) Sharron Denise McCain, born January 4, 1970: Sharron is divorced
  2) Brian Alan McCain, born December 2, 1974
Brian married Ashley Smiley McCain, September 7, 1996: Ashley Smiley was born
December 5, 1974
Brian and Ashley had two children:
       Karleigh Gabrielle Amille McCain, born July 16, 1997 and
       Jesse Brian Robert McCain, born November 29, 2000.
McCain and James:

    I am including here and in MY GRANDMOTHER'S BOOK a copy of a speech I made on October 13, 1989. Mama was living with me on Raymond Helms Road when I wrote and delivered this speech. She was my source of information and my inspiration.

"DOWN MEMORY LANE"

Presented October 13, 1989
Holiday Inn, Monroe, NC
North Carolina Society Daughters of the American Colonists

A TRIBUTE TO THE WOMEN IN MY FAMILY
WHO ARE RESPONSIBLE FOR MY BEING HERE TONIGHT

GLADYS McCAIN KERR
CHAIR OF THE CENTENNIAL YEAR
OF CELEBRATION FOR THE TOWN OF WAXHAW, NC

    Hurricane Hugo came with a wind and fury which changed our landscape and altered our all too busy lives. It uprooted our trees, damaged and destroyed our homes, cut off our electricity and telephones, and yes, the water supply for many of us in the country. The noise of the wind was deadening, and each crashing tree made us wonder if the house would be crushed. The darkness was a blessing. I am not "a tall" sure our hearts or nerves could have withstood those hours of destruction without the grace of God.

    When daybreak finally came, our fear changed to thanksgiving. Thanksgiving for our lives. Those who had battery operated radios learned a tiny baby had died in his crib when a tree fell on his room. Later we heard a man riding a motorcycle had been killed. Winds of almost a hundred miles an hour, torrential rains, and only two fatalities! Why did the huge trees fall to rest beside a house, a barn, an automobile? We shall never forget; we view life with sincere reverence and hope now. We are more forgiving and compassionate.

For months now I have planned to share the excitement of our Waxhaw Centennial Celebration. Waxhaw was founded March 7, 1889. On March 7, 1989, Governor James B. (Jim) Hunt addressed our Opening Ceremony. During the year we experienced a perfectly beautiful Fashion Show, depicting 100 years of Women's Fashions, the Waxhaw Woman's Club sponsored its Annual Antique Show, Two Antique and Craft Shows were held on the Village Green, and it was the 25th Year of our outdoor production *Listen and Remember*. We marched in a soggy but jubilant Fourth of July Parade. Camp Meeting at Pleasant Grove Camp Ground was extra special. There was the Annual Andrew Jackson Football Classic between NC and SC and, yet to come, the Dedication of the Restoration of the Waxhaw Well House, the Production of an Original Play *The Promised Land*, a community Thanksgiving Service, Christmas Caroling, a Teddy Bear Parade, Breakfast with Santa, and a Centennial Ball.

Can you believe a town of 1,400 people could muster enthusiasm and pride enough for a Whole Year? Reading old survey maps, searching for pictures, and clippings, and sharing stories of the past have been a memorable experience.

I also planned to relay memories of three trips, chaperoning college students to Philadelphia, Washington DC, New York City, and Boston. How thrilling to relive the early days of our ancestors as we read and studied prior to the actual trip. Walking the Freedom Trail, sitting in Constitution Hall, touching the Liberty Bell, visiting the homes of Paul Revere, Louisa Mae Alcott, Nathaniel Hawthorne, the Witches Museum of Salem--all these made history lessons come alive! We were overwhelmed by the courage, faith, and sacrifices of fellow Americans.

One hundred years ago, Victorian Elegance, before that perhaps a three-room farm house, and before that one room with a loft! During the ten days of darkness, with no water, not even any to be drawn from a well...I thought of my grandmothers, every day a challenge to survive: hostile Indians, unpredictable weather, preparing food and drink for large families. Did they make it because they were God-fearing women, church- going folk who valued education and integrity, or was it a stroke of luck?

There were good times: dinner on the grounds at church, box suppers at the school, quilting parties in homes, barn raisings, corn shuckings,---neighbor helping neighbor, families dedicated to hard work and serious about religion.

These last three weeks we saw this same spirit of sharing and caring as neighbors cut trees, patched roofs, replaced broken windows, mended broken fences, and shared generators to save food carefully stored in freezers. Children caught the spirit of community and few suffered for lack of a TV. When fire destroyed a home, churches organized assistance for the family.

It was early to bed and early to rise, candles, kerosene lamps, reflections of days gone by--walking, riding horseback, splitting wood, managing without indoor plumbing... but most important of all, we were alive; we were a real family, Dad, Mom, children, and grandchildren.

Were you lucky to be near grandparents when you were young? They had time for you: stories to tell and secrets to share, fishing, swimming, rocking on the porch, swinging in a hammock, lessons in how to pitch horse shoes, play marbles, thread a needle, piece a quilt, churn real butter, and singing and dancing in the parlor. HOW I REMEMBER SOUNDS AND SMELLS OF GRANDMA'S KITCHEN: STICKIES, HOREHOUND STICK CANDY, BLACKBERRY COBBLER, SCUPPERNONG WINE, THE STEREO-SCOPE (PICTURES ON A STICK), HAND CHURNED ICE CREAM, BLOCK ICE FOR YOUR SWEET TEA, COLD WATERMELON, HOT BISCUITS, HOMEMADE BUTTER, BANANA PUDDING, AND CHOCOLATE CAKE!

Suddenly, I was overcome by the true meaning of being a Daughter of the American Colonists. I wanted to know all I could about these women in my family, women who took a stand beside their men, braved the tribulations of the Atlantic Ocean to build a home and forge a new nation in a new world. I have asked questions, listened to sad and humorous tales, and longed to get a clearer impression of my grandmothers.

How amazed I was to learn Mary Eliza White Jolliff, my great-grandmother, packed her trunk and rode a stagecoach to New Garden Boarding School (now Guilford College). She remained in school in Greensboro for five years without coming home even once. (SHOW MARY ELIZA'S HAT, GLOVES, LACE, GRANDMA LELIA'S BELL)

Mary Eliza married a handsome, wealthy plantation owner, John Jolliff, a man who owned slaves, built her a lovely home with a long lane and English hedge rows. Her wedding gown had 30 yards of silk, grey, not white in color. She bore 17 children, three sets of twins, and only 2 girls and 3 boys survived. One daughter, my grandmother Lelia, was a teacher, and the youngest son Marvin was a Methodist preacher. This amazing woman loved to dance; she loved life. My Mama inherited her black straw Polk Bonnet, which cost $2.00. Now I treasure this heirloom.

Lelia Manola Jolliff Winslow, my grandmother, walked alone to Belvidere Academy for seven years. She left with her breakfast in her hand, and it was dark when she got home. Grandma Lelia won a speaking contest and won a silver medal with her name engraved on it. She taught 8 grades in a one-room school house for $25.00 a month. She walked 3 or 4 miles each day to teach. I have her school bell which she rang to begin the day and call the children in from recess. Grandma Lelia was a writer. She wrote poems about Death, Birth, Seasons, and Friends. I want to share her poem about her forty-fourth birthday.

BIRTHDAY MUSING BY LELIA MANOLA JOLLIFF WINSLOW June 13, 1869

I began my tiny life,
Nurtured by my mother kind,
I've lived to be a wife.
At twenty-one I was married
To a handsome, nice young man;
Away from home was carried
According to our plan.
In a cozy little home
We started life anew,
To take things as they come
With nothing ill in view.
I'm forty-four today...
Ten children have been ours,
Two are gone away
And are celestial flowers.
Eight are left...
the eldest twenty-two
The youngest now is eight;
I want them to be true
And enter Heaven's Gate.
Silver threads are in my hair,
Age is creeping on;
My brow is not so fair
As once to look upon.
But the love we bear each other
Is strong as iron bands,
The binding tie none can sever
In this, or other lands;
Down Life's stream we've been together
In scarcity and plenty, in fair and cloudy weather
Since I was one and twenty.
I've tried to live a good, true life
With Jesus for my Guide;
I've tried to be a faithful wife
Though often surely tried.
For mothers who their children love
Their passions must subdue,
And lift their thoughts above
To things which yet are true.

When I'm gone I hope they'll see
I taught them what was right,
I hope they will Christians be
Serve God with all their might.
Sunset of life will soon be here,
Evening-star a call for me,
I want no mourning at the pier
When I sail upon death's sea.
The boatman soon will come
Across the waters dark,
To take my spirit home
In eternity's able bark.
Hope shall my anchor be
Faith shall be my guide, I know that I shall see
Christ on the other side.
So...weep not when I embark
By twilight's evening star, Me thinks I hear the
music...Hark!
It seems not very far.
In readiness let me stand,
For the call that's sure to come,
From across the "Golden Strand,"
To waif my spirit home.

Lelia Jolliff had ten children and reared eight, one set of twins. When the twins arrived, her mother sent Aunt Caroline, one of her slaves who refused to leave after the Civil War, along with her husband, to help out! Grandma Lelia taught Sunday School. She was a good Methodist who later became a Quaker because the Friends' Church was nearer home. What a seamstress she was! She would go to Norfolk, look at the ready-made dresses, draw a sketch, go home, cut a pattern from newspaper and dress her girls in high fashion! She crocheted and tatted.

Memories of summer visits to Grandma Lelia's home include: her Bible on the dining room table, devotional at breakfast, salt herring for breakfast, the ice box, fresh milk and butter, fried chicken, baked ham, spoon bread, and pound cake. We three McCain children so looked forward to Grandma's wonderful letters to Mama which contained 10 cents each from her egg money for us. Grandma Lelia was so loving, so smart, and so wanted her children to be educated and prosperous.

Great-grandmother Martha Smith Copeland Winslow was tall and slender. She was a farmer's wife and the mother of eight. "Bee Taking" was a family affair. My Mama remembers going with her mother and dad to spend the night when bees were to be taken.

The bees had to be killed in order to take the honey. Another family visit was for "hog killing." It took two days and 30-35 hogs were slaughtered. The house was a two-story and had a breezeway connecting the kitchen to the rest of the house. The kitchen was a separate structure because there was a fear of fire. Grandma Martha had a red high chair for the littlest one! I have discover that Great-great Grandma Esther, called Easter, smoked a pipe!

Mary Elizabeth (Lizzie) Walkup McCain was a petite lady who at age 13, when her mother died, found herself in charge of the family. She loved to ride horseback, always side-saddle of course. Lizzie married at age 16 and due to the early death of her husband, with staunch courage, she managed the farm and reared seven of the nine children she bore. Granny Lizzie read, quilted, and remained faithful to Tirzah Presbyterian Church until her death. She and George Washington stopped the mail each year on February 22nd, for that was her birthday. She dipped snuff, and I have a snuff can. Granny Lizzie always wore a starched white apron which had a pocket for the snuff box and the sweet gum brush she used for dipping. One of her favorite sayings was, "A Have to is a Hard Way to Go." Her favorite desserts were banana pudding and cherry pie. She forever had a piece of pie in the pie safe. Her berry pies were carefully baked so you could hold a piece in your hand without making a mess! Granny cooked Sunday dinner on Saturday, and the family ate a cold meal after returning from church. Most of Sunday was spent going to, sitting in service, and coming back home.

While investigating for the Centennial, I discovered the home of Hugh McCain, my link to membership in Daughters of the American Revolution. We think this house may be one of the oldest in Union County. It was inhabited by family members until the 1940's. (It has been dismantled and parts moved to Concord, I think.) I did rescue a board from the house, which I cherish. Andrew Pickens and James Walkup's wife, Margaret Pickens Walkup, are my links to membership in Daughters of the American Colonists. Margaret Pickens was the second child of Israel Pickens whose father was Israel Sidney. The Pickens and Davis families came to America in 1736, landing at Paxton, near Philadelphia. The four families (Robert Davis, Robert, John and Andrew Pickens who was the father of Israel Pickens) moved to the frontier of August County, Virginia in 1730's and then in 1751 to Waxhaw settlement on the NC/SC line. Margaret Pickens was born about 1740 in the old Augusta County, Virginia and baptised by Rev. John Craig at the Stone Church on December 18,1740. She was the first cousin of the Revolutionary Major General Andrew Pickens. She died in Anson County. NC, on December 22, 1793. Her husband was Capt. James Walkup. They had the following children:

1. Samuel Walkup - b. 1758 - m. (1) Elizabeth Guthrie - m. (2) Nancy Patterson.
2. John Walkup - b. Dec. 6, 1760
3. James Walkup - b. Sept. 17, 1763 - d. March 30, 1784.
4. Martha Walkup - b. Feb. 10, 1766 - m. John Finley.

5. Israel Walkup - b. Sept. 17, 1768 - m. Peggy Morrow.
6. William Walkup - b. Nov. 22, 1770 - m. Hannah Orr.
7. Robert Walkup - b. Dec. 7, 1773 (another account says June 25, 1780 and died Sept. 22, 1846) - m. (1) Elizabeth Huey, m. (2) Dorcas Montgomery.
8. Jospeh Walkup - b. 1776 - m. Jane Orr.
9. Nancy (or Agnes) Walkup b. 1780 - m. William Crockett.
10. Margaret Walkup - b. Aug. 10, 1783 - m. William Brown.

Capt. James Walkup's home on Walkup Road still stands and is owned by Mrs. John (Claudia) Belk. Jane McCain, a distant relative, loaned William Henry Belk $500.00 to get his first store established in Monroe.

My mother, Isa Gladys Winslow McCain, was a teacher, bookkeeper for Daddy at the Farmers' Ginning and Trading Store, and Sunday School teacher. She was blessed with a beautiful voice, crocheted and tatted, loved all things beautiful, and was a gracious hostess. We had lots of company! Years before her marriage to Robert Maxwell McCain, Sr., she survived a serious operation and was told, "No children." Well, she became the mother of three, two girls and one boy, and eventually the grandmother of six handsome boys. Her handwriting is a work of art. She wrote poetry, as did her mother, and she was a medal winning orator. She encouraged excellence in all undertakings. Her buttermilk biscuits were prize winners.

Closing: I am a part of all these people: pointed nose, freckles, small hands, a thirst for learning, never afraid of hard work, a love of music, an appreciation of beauty created by God and man, a love for children, and compassion for all people!

When have you recently talked with your children and grandchildren about their heritage, especially about their grandmothers? When you snap beans, shell peas, sit on the porch, and rock in your favorite chair, REMEMBER. In your families there were women as lovely, sincere, and determined as Elizabeth Jackson, as patriotic as Betsy Ross, and as courageous as Molly Pitcher. A quote from *The Charlotte Observer,* September 3, 1989, sums this up: "The best talkers I know are women. I grew up with black women and white women telling stories, justifying themselves. Everybody knows the South is a matriarchy and the women are in control. The idea that men are in control is just a myth everybody agrees to pretend to." (Rocky Mount native Allan Gurganus, first novel *Oldest Living Confederate Widow Tells All.*)

Share these stories with the children. They will be enchanted, thirst for more, and hopefully, become Daughters of the American Colonists: PROUD AND DISTINGUISHED DAUGHTERS, WILLING TO WORK TO PRESERVE THE PAST, PRESENT, AND FUTURE.

REMAINDER OF PROGRAM

Guest Vocalist...Brenda J. Woodson

"Somewhere Over the Rainbow"..........................Harold Arlen

"Tribute to Waxhaw"............original composition by Krista Caryn Russell

Grandchildren of Robert Thompson McCain 2014: Bob, Gladys, Lynn, Lake, Cooper, Carole, Mildred, Bill, Myrtle, Dale, Jack, Joe

Gladys Kerr and brother Robert McCain

Gladys McCain Kerr and Mother Isa Gladys Winslow McCain with son James Kerr

The McCain-Winslow Connection

(The following is made up of excerpts from Wikipedia, research by genealogist Elizabeth Doherty Herzfeld of Boston who has written extensive about the Quakers and Southern Winslows, and research by other Winslows who have posted their findings at Ancestry. com. I leave the continued research to future family members who will add and correct the information here. At least you have a good starting place!)

John Winslow (1597–1674)

The McCains are connected to the Winslow family through my mother Isa Gladys Winslow McCain who married Robert Maxwell McCain, Sr. (1900-1984). She was the daughter of my grandfather Dempsey Eugene Winslow who was, as best I can determine, a descendant of the John Winslow who came to Plymouth Colony in 1621, following his brothers Edward and Gilbert who arrived a year earlier in 1620 as passengers on the *Mayflower*.

John Winslow (1597–1674) was one of several Winslow brothers who came to the Plymouth Colony. His brothers Edward and Gilbert were the first to arrive in 1620, and John followed in 1621 as a passenger on the *Fortune*. Two other brothers, Kenelm and Josiah, also settled in New England, arriving before 1632. The Winslow family was involved in all aspects of the Plymouth Colony, producing in the 17th century several governors and making their mark in New England history in both government and business. John Winslow was born April 16, 1597, in Droitwich, Worcestershire, England. He grew up in Droitwich, Worcestershire, residing there with his parents, Edward Winslow and Magdalene Oliver/ Ollyver, one step-brother, four brothers and two sisters. His father was a salt extractor.

John Winslow is next mentioned in the 1623 Division of Land, a single person with one acre assigned to him. In 1626 his name appears on the 53-name list of Purchasers, who were prominent colony men involved in Plymouth investments. Winslow is mentioned next in the 1627 Division of Cattle (also used as a quasi-census), his name appears on the list of Lot 3 with the Standish family and other Winslows, including his brother Edward and wife Susanna (White) and her sons by Pilgrim William White. Winslow's wife Mary and their son John appear on the list for Lot 6 with other families. He was declared a freeman in 1633 and became active in the government of the colony. On July 1, 1633, and again on January 3, 1636/37, the General Court ordered that the passage between Green's Harbor and the sea be enlarged, and the governor, and Assistants, and John Winslow and other prominent men were assigned to apportion costs to "every man" and to supervise the work there with ten men working at a time. On July 25, 1633, the court noted that John Beavan had covenanted to serve John Winslow as an apprentice for six years and at the end of the term Winslow was to give to him twelve bushels of Indian corn and twenty-five acres of land. On July 23, 1634, Mr. Timothy Hatherly turned over the remaining term of his servant Ephraim Tinkham to John Winslow, and Winslow was obligated to perform the conditions expressed in the indenture. On March 3, 1634, John Winslow was on a committee to assess colonists for the costs of the watch and other charges.

As early as January 5, 1635, John Winslow, his brother Kenelm Winslow, John Doane and other prominent men were chosen to assist the governor and council to set rates on goods to be sold and wages paid laborers. The court not only regulated prices, but sometimes quality. He is next mentioned on November 2, 1636, where he turned over the indentured services of Edmond Weston for two years to Nathaniel Thomas, on behalf of the latter's father, Mr. William Thomas. Monies and goods were to be exchanged in the process. Winslow was on the committee in 1637 to assess taxes for the cost of sending men to the Pequot War. Winslow continued to be very active in the colonial government, and in 1638 he and his brother Kenelm were witnesses against Stephen Hopkins for selling wine at excessive rates.

Many of the more prosperous men had indentured servants. John Winslow was one of them. Records show that on July 28, 1640, he sold for £12 the services of Grosse for five years to John Howland. On yet another important committee, on October 17, 1642, Winslow was noted as one of several men appointed to grant lands for the town of Plymouth, and in the 1643 he is listed among the "Men Able to Bear Arms." He appears with the men of Plymouth. He also served for two years as Deputy from Plymouth to the general court, and in 1653 Winslow became a member of "a counsell of war" (Council of War). Winslow was well thought of and a man to be trusted as evidenced in a record which shows that on March 20, 1654, Stephen Tracy, who had returned to England and was residing at Great Yarmouth in Norfolk, gave power of attorney to John Winslow of Plymouth to dispose of his estate in New England for the benefit of his son John Tracy, daughters Ruth Tracy and Mary Tracy, and the rest of his five children. John Tracy married Mary Prence, daughter of Governor Thomas Prence.

On October 10, 1657, John Winslow of Plymouth sold all his house and land in Plymouth to Edward Gray, believed to be his son-in-law married to his daughter Mary, and moved to Boston, where he became a wealthy merchant and ship owner, as well as retaining some land in Plymouth. Winslow held the distinction of being on the 1662 list of "first born" men of Plymouth to share in a land distribution, and he was one of the witnesses to the sale of land by Myles Standish in 1661. On September 19, 1671, it is recorded that John bought for the sum of £500 in New England silver money "the Mansion or dwelling-house of the Late Antipas Voice with the gardens wood-yard and Backside as it is situate lying and being in Boston aforesaid as it is now fenced in And is fronting & Facing to the Lane going to Mr. John Jolliffe's." The Winslows lived in this house until his death in 1674 and that of Mary Chilton in 1679. The house (which would have been on Spring Lane) no longer exists.

John Winslow married Mary Chilton between 1623 and May 22, 1627 in Plymouth and had ten children. She had been baptized in St. Peter's Parish, Sandwich, Kent, England, on May 31, 1607, and she died between July 31, 1676, and May 1, 1679, in Boston. In 1620

Mary and her parents had come to Plymouth as passengers on the *Mayflower*. Her parents died the first winter. Her father James Chilton is named on several memorials in Province-town in honor of those who were the earliest to die on board the *Mayflower* in November and December 1620.

Children of John and Mary Winslow, all born in Plymouth after May 22, 1627

John was born about 1627 and died in Boston between October 3 and 12, 1683. His name appears with his mother Mary on the 1627 Division of Cattle list for Plymouth, with the father John named on a separate list. He married (1) Elizabeth _____ before April 18, 1664 (birth of first child) and had four children, all born in Boston. No record of her after August 7, 1670. (2) Judith _____ after August 7, 1670. She was born about 1625 and died shortly before December 18, 1714 (burial date), in Boston, age near 90. John and Mary's children were as follows:

Susanna was born about 1630 and died after November 14, 1685, in East Bridgewater. She married Robert Latham by 1650 and had eight children, probably born in Bridgewater. He was possibly born in England about 1613 and died in Bridgewater at age 76. Both were buried in Old Grave Yard, East Bridgewater, Section B. Reports from the records of the Plymouth coroner's jury on January 31, 1654, details an event that is termed one of the most extreme cases of a master mistreating a servant in that colony. This involved Susanna and her husband Robert Latham. From the records the case details a systemic abuse of 14 year old John Walker, apparently an indentured servant, who died with a battered, bruised, starved and frozen body at the fault of his master and mistress. His master Robert Latham admitted whipping him "all his backe with stripes given him by his master, Robert Latham, as Robert himself did testify," and testimony from witnesses revealed that "he (Latham) gave John Walker some stripes that morning before his death; and also we find the flesh much broken of the knees of John Walker, and that he did want sufficient food and clothing and lodging." On March 4, 1654, Robert Latham was indicted for felonious cruelty to his servant John Walker by unreasonable correction, by withholding necessary food and cloth-ing, and by exposing Walker to extremities of the seasons, whereby he died. The trial jury found him guilty of "manslaughter by chaunce medley" and he was sentenced to be burned in the hand, and having no lands, to have all his personal property confiscated. Latham's wife Susanna was presented by the grand jury for being in great measure guilty with her husband in exercising extreme cruelty toward their late servant John Walker.

Mary was born about 1631 and died after October 28, 1663, and before November 1665 in Plymouth. She married Edward Gray on January 16, 1650, and had six children, all born in Plymouth. Edward Gray, born about 1629, is recorded as being a merchant and among the wealthiest of Plymouth Colony. He remarried in December 1665 Dorothy Lettice and had six more children. Edward Gray died in Plymouth in June 1681 at age 52.

Edward was born about 1635-36 and died in Boston on November 19, 1682. He was likely buried in Copps Hill Burying Ground, Boston, with his first wife Sarah. He married (1) Sarah Hilton by 1661 and had three children born in Boston. She died on April 4, 1667, in Boston, age 26. (2) Elizabeth Hutchinson on February 8, 1668, and had five children born in Boston. She died September 16, 1728, in Boston in her 89th year.

Sarah was born about 1638-39 and died on April 9, 1726, in Boston at age 88. She married (1) Myles Standish, Jr., on July 19, 1660. He disappeared at sea after March 20, 1661. He was a son of Pilgrim Myles Standish. They had no children. She married (2) Tobias Payne in 1667 and had one son William born in Boston. Payne died in Boston on September 12, 1669. She married (3) Richard Middlecott in 1672 and had four children. He was born in England about 1640 and died on June 13, 1704, in Boston.

Samuel was born about 1641 and died in Boston on October 14, 1680, at age 39. He married Hannah Briggs before June 22, 1675. and had two children baptized in Scituate. Hannah married (2) Capt. Thomas Jolls. She died after November 4, 1714, in Boston. Samuel was buried in Copps Hill Burying Ground, Boston

Isaac was born about 1643-44 and died at Port Royal, Jamaica, between August 26 and 29, 1670. He married Mary Nowell on August 14, 1666, and had two children born in Charlestown. Mary later married in 1674 John Long with whom she had four children. She died before January 23, 1729, in Charlestown.

<u>JOSEPH WINSLOW</u> was a mariner and the ancestor of Isa Gladys Winslow McCain. He was born about 1645 and died before August 7, 1679, as he is mentioned in the will of his mother Mary Winslow with his inheritance going to his children. He either died on Long Island, New York or had moved to NC and is most likely the Winslow who owned lands in North Carolina, served on a jury in 1676. He was married to Sarah Lawrence (b. 1642 Plymouth) about 1668 and had four children. Sarah married (2) Charles LeBros. She died before 1693. A child was born about 1651 and died young, certainly before March 12, 1673 (date of father's will).

Benjamin was born on 12 August 1653 in Plymouth. He died between 12 March 1673 and 31 July 1676. He was unmarried.

The Will of John Winslow

The will of John Winslow, Sr., of Boston, merchant and father of Joseph, was dated 12 March 1673/74, and proved 31 May 1674. In the will he named his wife Mary, sons John, Isaac, Benjamin, Edward, and William Payne, the son of his daughter Sarah Middlecott;

Parnell Winslow, daughter of his son Isaac; granddaughter Susanna Latham; son Edward's children; son **Joseph Winslow**'s two children ("Item I give unto my sone **Joseph Winslow**'s two Children five pounds pr peece to be paid unto them as afforesaid"); granddaughter Mercy Harris's two children; kinsman Josiah Winslow "now governor of New Plimouth"; brother Josiah Winslow; kinswoman Eleanor Baker, the daughter of his brother Kenelm Winslow; "my seven children"; Mr. Paddy's widow; and his Negro girl Jane. He left personal property valued at £3,000, a good part of it in money, and this was a substantial sum for the time. He died between 12 March 1673/4 and 21 May 1674 in Boston, Massachusetts Bay Colony. At the time of his death he was one of the wealthiest merchants in Boston. Both he and his wife were buried in King's Chapel Burying Ground in Boston. They both left wills that survive today. His widow Mary survived him but died before May 1678, and she dated her will, equally as detailed as her husband's, 31 July 1676, proved 11 July 1679.

The Descendants of John Winslow and His Son Joseph of Massachusetts
(Each generation is underlined below that connects to McCain)

<u>JOSEPH WINSLOW</u> b. Plymouth Colony, Massachusetts, 1645. He had died by 7 August 1679, in either Long Island, NY, or Perquimans County, NC. Married Sarah Lawrence about 1668. Sarah died about 1693. One of their sons was Timothy Winslow who lived in Perquimans County, NC. <u>**TIMOTHY WINSLOW**</u> was born about 1655. Timothy died about 1706 in North Carolina. Timothy married Sarah, born about 1664. He contributed money to build the first Quaker Meeting House in Perquimans County, North Carolina. Timothy also paid a corn tax during the Tuscarora War. Timothy and Sarah signed with their marks as witnesses to both the marriage of their sons Thomas and John Winslow.

1. Thomas Winslow was born on 1 Aug. 1682 in Pasquotank County, North Carolina. He died on 26 Nov. 1745 in Perquimans County, North Carolina. Thomas married (1) Elisabeth CLARE daughter of Timothy CLARE and Mary BUNDY on 2 Nov. 1704 in Perquimans County. Elisabeth was born on 21 Feb. 1685/6 in Perquimans. She died before June 1734 in Perquimans County.

2. <u>**JOHN WINSLOW**</u> was born about 1685. He died on 25 Jan. 1753. Born in Pasquotank County, North Carolina. John married Esther SNELLING daughter of Israel SNELLING and Hannah LAWRENCE in 1716 in Perquimans County. Esther was born on 20 Sept. 1699 in Berkeley, North Carolina. She died after 14 Aug. 1755 in Perquimans. Esther was the stepsister of Elizabeth Clare, who married John Winslow's brother, Thomas. John received a land patent 9 November 1730 of 400 acres in Perquimans precinct, joining the land of Timothy Winslow's, probably the son of Thomas and Elizabeth, who had inherited the land from his grandfather, Timothy Clare, in 1724. Known children of John Winslow and Esther Snelling were as Kanan 1716, Israel 1717, Hannah 1727, Benjamin 1730 , **John 1733**, Elizabeth 1736, Joseph 1735, and Esther 1738. Their son <u>**JOHN WINSLOW**</u> was born

about 1733 and died 8 Feb. 1801 in Perquimans County, North Carolina, where he is listed on the 1790 Census. John married Rachel White 10 March 1752, in Perquimans County. She was the daughter of Thomas White and Rachel Jordan. Rachel White was the twin of Thomas White and sister of Mary White, who married Winslow, son of Winslow and Pleasant Tomes. Rachel's father was the son of John White of Isle of Wright County, Virginia. Her mother was the daughter of Joshua Jordan and Elisabeth Sanbourne, daughter of Daniel and Sarah Sanbourne. Three of John and Rachel Winslow children were the following:

--Ann Winslow b. 12 Oct 1761, m. John Saunders 3 Dec. 1777 (Perquimans)
--John Winslow b. 15 Oct 1763, Perquimans, m. Margaret Bell 24 Nov. 1782, Perquimans.
--**SAMUEL WINSLOW** b. 3 December 1764. Perquimans, NC. Married Mary Ann White. Died Nov. 10, 1828 in Perquimans.   One of their sons was
Timothy Winslow born about 1804- died 1839.

Additional research indicates the Samuel's son **TIMOTHY WINSLOW** (b. about 1804-d. about 1839) married on 15 April 1829 Esther Jane White (1811-1896). She is listed as a widow on the 1880 Census of Perquimans County. Their son **Dempsey Evans Winslow** was born about 1838 and died 1917 in Up River, Perguimans County, NC. He married Martha Copeland b. 1837. Their son was **Dempsey Eugene Winslow** (1866-1948) who married Lelia Jolliff, the parents of **Isa Gladys Winslow McCain.**

The Winslow-McCain Connection:
Grandparents Dempsey and Lelia Jolliff Winslow

My grandmother was Lelia Manola Jolliff Winslow who was born June 30, 1869. On November 26, 1890, she married Dempsey Eugene Winslow who was born on September 12, 1866. This fine lady was stately, almost regal, very intelligent, talented, and a loving, devoted Christian. Her mother, Mary Eliza White, rode on a stage coach to New Garden Boarding School (Guilford College) in Greensboro, and stayed for five years. She was also very intelligent. Her husband was John Jolliff, quite a handsome, plantation owner with several slaves. When Grandma Lelia had twin boys, Earl and Percy, my great-grandmother Elizabeth White Jolliff sent her slave, Aunt Caroline and her husband, maybe Uncle Billy, to live with Grandma Lelia. They had quarters off the kitchen, which was a separate building, joined to the main house by a narrow porch.

The 1870 US Census for Belvidere Township in Perquimans County, (located in the Albemarle Sound region of NC) lists the family members of Dempsey Evans Winslow including Dempsey Eugene Winslow age three who would later marry Lelia Jolliff. Family members were-

Name	Age
Dempsey Evans Winslow	31
Martha Winslow	32
Sarah E Winslow	11
Henry E Winslow	9
Martha D Winslow	7
Dempsey Eugene Winslow	**3**
Elbert L Winslow	1
Mary Ann Perry	41

The Reverend K. Riddick, a Methodist minister of the Virginia Conference, officiated at the wedding of my grandparents. Grandpa Genie had build their home himself, so they moved right in. Aunt Eunice inherited the home and the farm, because she and Uncle Arba moved in to care for them in the 1940's. Initially, Aunt Mary did their laundry and Aunt Lessie (Atlessa) had prepared room for them at her home in Bagley Swamp. Neither grandparent wanted to leave home. It was so sad. Uncle Earl and his sons had continued to help Grandpa Eugene to farm. Uncle Worth, who drove an Allied Moving Van truck from east coast to west coast, was very angry. He came around later. I heard my mother Isa say she inherited $500 which she spent for her sterling silver, Chantilly. Carole, Drake, and I all chose this pattern and my daughter-in-law Dana chose Chantilly as well. That choice made me very happy.

My Grandma Lelia copied birthdays of her family on a decorative scroll. This piece of art is in my possession. It reads as follows:

Dempsey Eugene Winslow was born September 12, 1866 and died February 6, 1948. He married Lelia Manola Jolliff on November 26, 1890.
Lelia Manola Jolliff was born June 30, 1869 and died January 27, 1948.
They were blessed with ten children, two of whom died as babies.
The eight remaining children:
1. **Eunice Evelyn Winslow** was born September 25, 1891. Married Arba Elihu Winslow on December 24, 1913, at her home. Died August 21, 1976
2. Twins: Eugene Earl and **Percy Emmett Winslow** were born March 18, 1894. Earl married Mary Amelia Winslow September 16, 1914. Earl died July 20, 1972
3. **Percy Winslow** married Irene Winslow, December 20, 1916: second marriage: Nora White on October 18, 1922. Died March 1985
4. **Mary Susie Winslow** was born April 6, 1896, Married Lucious E. Winslow, November 25, 1914, at her home. Died June 1985
5. **Lelia Novella Winslow** was born December 11, 1897. Married Wayland White, May 18, 1914. Died March 17, 1955
6. **Elbert Worth Winslow** was born September 23, 1899. Married Nettie Ashley June 8, 1929 (Mama was in this wedding). Died September 25, 1967
7. **Isa Gladys Winslow** was born August 28, 1903. Married Robert Maxwell McCain, Sr.

November 23, 1932. Died February 9, 1993

8. **Atlessa (Lessie) Leanna Winslow** was born June 22, 1905. Married Joseph Winslow June 7, 1927. Died May 4, 1989.

The parents of Dempsey Eugene Winslow were Dempsey Evans Winslow and Martha S. Copeland Winslow. Both parents were born and died in Perquimans County, NC. The father was born May 28, 1838 and died May 19, 1917. His wife Martha was born October 13, 1837, and died March 1, 1910.

Their children listed by birth and death were as follows:

Sarah Elizabeth Winslow Layden 1859 – 1944

Henry Edgar Winslow 1860 – 1880

Martha Delphina "Dillie" Winslow Winslow 1862 – 1951

Dempsey Eugene Winslow 1866 – 1948

Elbert Lafayette Winslow 1869 – 1949

Lindley Jay Winslow 1871 – 1960

Arthur Neureus Winslow 1874 – 1946

Ira Sankey Winslow 1879 – 1961

Let me tell you about Grandma and Grandpa Winslow's house. As best I can remember, here is the floor plan: downstairs a short hall separated the master bedroom on the right from the living room on the left; the stairs went up on the living room side, several steps, a landing, a turn, and more steps; there was a closet under the stairs. Back to the hall, walk a few steps and you bump into a screen door and you are on the back porch where we ate, played and drank water from the pump at the end of the porch. A screen door led to the outside near the sink with the pump. Back to the living room which was used just for "company"; it was here on the sofa I looked at all those pictures of the world using the viewing headgear which made me look like an astronaut. Go through the door and you are in the dining room where we enjoyed so many outstanding meals and lingered to visit (I well remember the little wooden ice chest which had doors, shelves, and a place for a block of ice. How great the tea was with this chipped ice). Go on through the door and you are in the kitchen with its big wood-burning stove that Mama said cooked the best biscuits. (When all those children came home from school, Grandma would bake biscuits for their snack!) Food occupies my memories of being at Grandma's house. I so loved the spoon bread, a kind of corn bread made with meal and flour. How I adored Aunt Eunice's angel food cake. Fried chicken, fried fish, pot roast, fresh vegetables, and desserts galore! Mama inherited Grandma Lelia's dough tray; a long wooden tray with handles on each end. Think what stories that biscuit tray could tell! There was a long table where we ate and played and visited. In the kitchen there were two chairs at each end of the table (for Grandma and Grandpa). The children sat on two benches placed on either side of the table. My Mama said at Christmas Grandma Lelia would make as many as ten cakes. In addition, she would boil an entire "green" country ham. I remember the well in the pasture near the back door. It had a long pole with a bucket on the end which you let down into a rather shallow well. The water never tasted very good to me. I liked milk, cokes, and iced tea much better. The hen house was near the house. Remember the letters with egg money inside for the three of Isa's children! There was a big barn a little way back in the pasture. The pigs ran wild in the woods, I think. There was a smoke house behind the house with barrels of pickled herring and country hams. I do not recall that Grandma had fine china, crystal, or sterling, but she had some lovely serving pieces. My Mama inherited the Blue Willow Tea Pot, which I think belonged to the two sisters who lived in the house where Uncle Percy and Johnnie lived. Robert, my brother, was playing baseball in the house and broke the lid to that precious tea pot. I am now the happy owner of the pot with no lid.

Now back to the front porch: there were rocking chairs and a hydrangea bush near the steps. I would practice jumping over the bush into the front yard. Marjorie Blanchard reminded me of the two huge trees in the front yard. Marjorie reported the entire family had the best picnic meals out in the yard under those trees, at least twice a year. Since my Daddy had to stay in Waxhaw and work, he wrote lots of letters. I loved running to the mail box just at the edge of the front yard, which had no grass, just sand, to get news from Daddy. Another past-time for me was to stand on a chair in the hall and peer out the colored glass windows on each side of the front door. There were pink, blue, green, and yellow panes in the window. For me it was seeing the world through "rose-colored glasses."

Before I forget, Mama told me about hog killing at her Grandfather Dempsey Evans Winslow's home. A huge number were slaughtered in a day. Family and neighbors came to help. Lard for cooking was boiled from the fat; the meat was cut into pork chops, hams and shoulders for frying, and sausage was ground. There was a Red High Chair which the younger grandchildren got to sit in while the grown-ups worked. Mama loved that chair.

After rearing eight children, Grandma Lelia began to have cerebral hemorrhages. She always worn her hair long, platted in a pig tail, and wrapped around her head. She was tall, refined, carried herself well, and was most cordial. The strokes left her unable to comb or brush her hair, so Grandpa did this for her. Their love was so strong and sure; it made everyone around them warm and comfortable. Mama took the bus home to Belvidere, NC, when Grandma was so sick the last time. Grandma Lelia died on January 27, 1948. I was in the eighth grade and Granny Lizzie McCain, Daddy's Mama, came to be with Robert, Carole, and me. Grandpa had not left Grandma for a minute. He was stricken with pneumonia and was too ill to attend her funeral. He died ten days later.

Earlier I mentioned my grandparents were married by a Methodist minister. They attended Bethany Methodist Church which was a distance from their farm. Riding in a cart or wagon was not so pleasant. The Up River Friends (Quaker) Church was to the left of the farm and at the end of their road. Thus, for convenience, they became members of this congregation. Leslie Winslow, my first cousin, son of Lucious and Mary Winslow, became a Quaker minister. His wife, Ruby Smith, was an elementary school teacher and a member of *Delta Kappa Gamma* Society. The only pastor I knew at Up River Church was Cousin Elizabeth (Lizzie)

White, who lived across the road in front of Grandma and Grandpa's house. I remember her house: white, attractive on the outside, but inside was a narrow hallway, dark and musty. As Cousin Lizzie grew older, she looked forward and perhaps expected, Grandpa to deliver her meals cooked by my Grandmother each day. Women and men sat in separate sections of the church. There was no singing, no music, only Quiet. I bet this was hard for the children.

I never quite understood the order of worship at Up River Quaker Meeting House. Having Lizzie White in the pulpit was different. There was a great deal of scripture reading, a sermon, and prayers. But as the years passed, there was music, even an organ. My cousin by marriage, Johnnie White, Aunt Nora's daughter, played the organ. She was a distinguished school teacher, dressed professionally, and was well mannered and educated. When she died, her request was for me to play for her funeral. I did! Johnnie and Bill Winslow's wife, Marjorie, were dear friends. Many times Marjorie drove Johnnie to her doctor.

Great-Grandmother Mary Eliza White

As I reported earlier, Mary Eliza White, my great-grandmother, spent five years at boarding school in Greensboro. Grandma Lelia allowed Mama to have Mary Eliza's Sunday hat, a black straw Polk Bonnet which cost two dollars. Now that bonnet is mine, and I wear it when I am asked to speak about Grandma and her One-Room School House. Mary Eliza's daughter, Lelia, my grandmother, taught school in a one-room school house. She had eight grades and was the only teacher to finish the eighth grade arithmetic book. The chairman of the school board lived next-door to the one room wooden school building. He would stand in the yard to be sure Grandma Lelia never allowed the children to overstay their outside recess period. I do believe she walked about 5 miles to school with her breakfast in her hand. She had to draw water from the well so the children would have a drink from the common dipper. She also made a fire in the little pot-bellied stove. Perhaps the big boys had brought in wood the afternoon before, or maybe she fetched the wood herself! The children sat on benches and wrote on slates. She loved her work; she loved the children; and most of all she LOVED LEARNING. Grandma Lelia gave my Mama her school bell. Now I own that bell.

Aunt Eunice taught at Belvidere, I think. I am not sure about whether she went to college, ever. Aunt Lessie went to Guilford College while Mama taught to help pay her tuition. Then Aunt Lessie taught so Mama could go to Guilford. Mama loved to tell me about her French professor; that lady spoke French always, which made Mama learn to speak the language faster. Mama never liked math, but she loved English, history, and her plan was to teach in the elementary school. Mama told me often about Miss Pearl White who was her early teacher at Whiteston Elementary. Miss Pearl's house was near the Up River Friend's Church. I do believe I actually met her. Let me tell you a little more about my Mama and her school children. I think she taught at Bethel and maybe at Tarboro, where she lived in a teacherage. Each place Mama taught she made lasting friends. While attending summer school at East Carolina, she met Kate Griffin from Wingate, NC. Kate encouraged Mama to apply for a position at Waxhaw, NC. which she did. She got the job, got married, and lived to be almost

90! Most recently I found an envelope with pictures of all the students Mama had in a second grade class at Waxhaw. Reby loved to tell me how she rode in the cart, driving the horse herself, her destination was Grandma Lelia's to prepare for Isa's company. There was cleaning and cooking to be done. Reby was instructed by Grandma to put clean sheets on the beds, fold the top sheets down and put a few drops of Evening in Paris perfume on the corner of the sheets!

Grandma Lelia's Sewing Ability

My Grandma Lelia's sewing machine was given to my Mama, Isa. Grandma made all the girls' clothes and Mama made many of mine. I feel sure Grandma made wedding dresses for Eunice, Mary, and Novella. My Mama bought a beautiful dark blue velveteen long gown for her wedding. I still have this wedding dress, along with her night gown, which I keep in the cedar chest drawer of Mama's chest of drawers. Now, I do remember the story of Aunt Eunice's wedding dress. Mama had the wedding picture of Aunt Eunice and Uncle Arba, and it is hanging over Mama's chest of drawers. Look carefully at Aunt Eunice's lovely white dress. Grandma Lelia went to Norfolk, walked the streets looking in the windows at the fancy dress shops. She took pen and paper and sketched pictures of the ones she liked. Grandma came home, cut out a pattern from newspaper, and sewed this lovely dress for Aunt Eunice. She also made beautiful quilts. I have the tulip quilt she made for my Mama when she married on November 23, 1932. It is so old and a little ragged, but please, Mc-Cain, save it and remember the occasion. Grandma also crocheted, and maybe tatted. My Mama could crochet so beautifully. I have the table cloth she started when I was a baby. She never finished it, but I used it for a runner on the dining table. Grandma made a bedspread with those loopers. Each square looks like a pot holder. It has fringe on the edges. It is in the guest room closet. Protect it, please. Mama learned how to tat from a pen pal friend of Grandma's, named Isa. This lady came to Belvidere to visit one summer and taught Mama this unique art. Mama made the most baby slips, pillow cases, table cloths, collars, and trim for dresses. I feel Mama was hoping for a granddaughter to wear those little slips made with lace and love, but she and Daddy had six fine grandsons and later four great-granddaughters, plus seven great-grandsons. Oh, how proud I am of these ladies. Mama tried to teach me to do "fancy work," but I was impossible. I barely learned to put in a hem!

April 25, 2015

McCain,

I do believe I have about finished your book. Please read it now and then, just to remember those who came before you. Maybe you will laugh, or even shed a tear, but do always be proud of who you are! Never forget, your Nina loves you to the moon and back!

McCain Dates to Remember
Copied from the script used at Walkersville Presbyterian Church
A Day to Honor Grandpa and Granny McCain

Robert Thompson McCain's father was Alexander Maxwell McCain, born October 8, 1820.
Grandpa "Bob" Robert Thompson McCain (Born April 24, 1860) (Died June 11, 1927)
Granny Lizzie, Mary Elizabeth Walkup McCain (Born February 22, 1868)
(Died March 24, 1953)
They married on February 7, 1884: Granny was 16 and Grandpa was almost 24.
They had nine children: two died as infants. They are buried at Tirzah Presbyterian Church with Granny and Grandpa. James will bury my ashes in their plot.

Their Children Who Lived

1. **Mary Margaret Elizabeth McCain Norwood** (Born August 30, 1885)
(Died June 10, 1972)
Married Alphonzo Berge Norwood November 6, 1907
Alphonzo Berge Norwood (Born January 8, 1884) (Died November 10, 1949)
Seven children were born to this marriage, 4 boys and 3 girls.
Their children were as follows:
a. Robert Wilson Norwood (Born September 24, 1908) (Died April 1, 1984)
Married Nellie Simpson Norwood October 26, 1940
Nellie Simpson Norwood (Born September 1, 1915 or 1916) (Died August 30, 2000)
1 child was born to this marriage, a boy, Wilson Walker Norwood (Born May 31, 1941)
Walker's Wife: Patsy Jane Harrell (Born May 31, 1948) (Living) Married July 31, 1971
Walker and Patsy have one child: Patty Lydia Norwood (Born September 7, 1979)
Patty has five children:
b. Ellen Belk Norwood Baker (Born September 2, 1911) (Died March 28, 2004)
Married Paul Hueston Baker April 15, 1933
Paul Baker (Born May 7, 1905) (Died December 17, 1982)
Two children were born to this marriage, both girls: Mary Dannie Baker (Born July 2, 1936)
Dannie's husband: Harold Jake Vaughn (Born January 25, 1932) Married June 2, 1956
Dannie and Harold have four children: Della, Cathy, Jay, and Amy
Ellen Elizabeth Baker (Born October 4, 1954)
Ellen Elizabeth's husband: Howard Pearson West (Born April 26, 1946)
Married October 15, 1986
Ellen Elizabeth and Howard have two children: Matthew Howard West (Born May 7, 1989)
 and Baker Andrew West (born December 16, 1991)
c. Cooper Elizabeth Norwood Starnes (Born August 21, 1914) (Died April 3, 2008)
Married Brascus Harrison "Jack" Starnes October 14, 1933
Jack Starnes (Born October 16, 1911) (Died September 19, 1976)

Three children were born to this marriage, 2 boys: Albert and Alfonzo, and 1 girl: Libby

d. Myrtle Gryder Norwood Simpson (Born June 29, 1917) (Died March 13, 2003)

Married Simmie Hazel Simpson, Sr. October 8, 1939

Simmie Simpson (Born April 14, 1914) (Died January 15, 1981)

Two children were born to this marriage, 1 boy: Hazel and 1 girl: Phyllis

e. William Franklin "Bill" Norwood (Born May 25, 1920) (Died September 25, 1990)

Married Ruth McManus Norwood March 11, 1945

Ruth McManus Norwood (Born October 25, or 2, 1925) (Living)

Four children were born to this marriage, 3 boys and 1 girl.

f. Samuel Blanton "Pete" Norwood (Born November 9, 1922 (Died April 9, 1963)

Married Maude Stewart Norwood in 1947

Maude Stewart Norwood (Born November 20, 1922) (Died January 24, 2000)

Three children were born to this marriage, 2 boys and 1 girl.

g. Jack Newton Norwood (Born September 18, 1926) (Died October 28, 2007)

Married Maxine Stewart Norwood February 4, 1950

Maxine Stewart Norwood (Born ?) (Died March 3, 2008)

Two children were born to this marriage, 1 boy and 1 girl.

2. **Samuel Hosea McCain** (Born May 27, 1890-Died March 28, 1968)

Married Kate Elizabeth Haigler McCain December 28, 1909

Kate Haigler McCain (Born June 14, 1892-Died June 16, 1970)

Three children were born to this marriage, 1 boy, Harold and 2 girls, Mary Lee and Geraldine.

CHILDREN

a. Mary Lee McCain Chandler (Born October 18, 1910) (Died September 3, 1992)

Married Arlis Clayton Chandler November 24, 1928

Arlis Clayton Chandler (Born December 4, 1906) (Died June 5, 1953)

b. Edna Geraldine McCain Brady (Born March 8, 1914) (Died Jan. 11. 2010)

Married Cyrus Lamar Brady July 22, 1932

Cyrus Brady (Born September 12, 1914) (Died May 14, 1974)

Three children were born to this marriage, 3 boys: Melvin Ott (1933-2003), Cyrus Lamar, (1937-2006), and Louis Gehrig (1943-2013)

Melvin married Rachel Gordon (b. May 20, 1936). Their children are Monte Brady (b. April 13, 1957) and Cathy Brady Greene (b. Aug. 21, 1959)

Cathy has three children: Krista Griffin (b. July 22, 1957), Kayla Funderburk (b. Nov. 12, 1991), and Colton Greene (b. Dec. 12 1995)

Rachel and Melvin's granddaughter Kayla married Cam Funderburk (b. July 10, 1984)

Krista m. Chris Griffin (b. 1979). Their children are Kinsley (b. Nov. 16, 2012) and Kaslyn Griffin b.May 1, 2015

Lamar has one daughter Beth Clark (b. May 5, 1964). Her daughter is Alison Clark (b. Oct. 24, 2004) Lamar's other grandchildren are Will Wilson (b. Sept. 9, 1990), Brady Wilson (b. Aug. 27, 1993), and Laken Wilson b. Sept. 26, 1985

Lou Brady has one daughter Rhonda Brady McManus who married Terry McManus. Their children are Tarah and Savannah. Tarah married Chris Helms and their children are Bryleigh Helms and Jase Helms.

c. Robert Harold McCain (Born May 20, 1916) (Died October 28, 1961)
Married Mary Lee Gordon McCain May 22, 1937
Mary Lee Gordon McCain (Born September 8, 1916-17) (Died   2005)
One child was born to this marriage, 1 girl, Jane (Born 1944) (Died 1963)

3. **Ella Jane McCain Helms** (Born May 28, 1893) (Died January 23, 1981)
Mahlon Alexander Helms (Born June 24, 1888) (Died July 16, 1968)
Married January 10, 1910
Seven children were born to this marriage, 4 boys and 3 girls
Their children were as follows:
a. *Lucille Elizabeth Helms Weddle* (Born April 28, 1911) (Died November 3, 1981)
Married Alexander Roosevelt (Eck) Weddle, April 1932 (Born September 30, 1902)
(Died January 8, 1974). Six children were born to this marriage, 2 boys and 4 girls
Their first child was Elizabeth Ann Weddle (Born) April 22, 1933
m. Roy C. Sappenfield June 4, 1956. Roy died May 20,1989. One child was born to
this marriage: Charlotte Annette Sappenfield (Born) May 1, 1960
Lucille and Eck's second child was Sarah Benson Weddle (Born) November 28, 1934
(Died) October 30, 1991. Married Myrties Russell April 10, 1955 (Died 1982)
Three children were born to this marriage: 1. Myrties Steve Russell (Born) August 25, 1956
2. Donna Gail Russell Edenburn (Born November 5, 1957). Married James Edenburn.
who was born Aug. 12, 1978. They had two children Triston Dawn Edenburn b. Mar. 9, 2002,
and Steven James Edenburn b. June 9, 2011
3. Wanda Kay Russell Rosenburger (Born) June 28, 1959.
Married Paul Rosenburger. Their one daughter is Ashley, born June 29, 1986
Ashley married Shawn Ace. Their children are Austin Paul Ace b. June 19, 2007
and Molly Marie Ace b. Feb. 2, 2009
Lucille and Eck's third child was Mary Alice Weddle (Born) August 20, 1937
Married John Glenn Bass, February 23, 1957. Three children were born to this marriage:
1. Mary Angela Bass Mitchell (Born) May 18, 1961
Married Anthony Mitchell: Mary and Anthony had one son, Jonathan (Born) May 25, 1986
Jonathan married Evalina Mitchell. Their children are Mila Leiana Mitchell b. Sept, 17 2009
and Saphya Averie Mitchell b. Oct. 18, 2012
2. Leigh Anne Bass Hammer (Born) March 24, 1963
Married Philip Hammer: Leigh Anne and Philip had daughters Katherine Leigh
b. October 6, 1995, and Jennifer Lynn b. March 20, 1998
3. Mary and John's son, John Kevin Bass was born June 5, 1975
Lucille and Eck's fourth child was Jerry Stuart Weddle (Born) September 21, 1939

(Died March 9, 1970). Married Benda Poplin Weddle (now a Thomas) Sept. 1963. No children.

Lucille and Eck's fifth child was David Alexander Weddle (Born) April 11, 1942
Married Barbara Anne Jones Weddle on February 14, 1971. She was born
March 24, 1947. Two children were born to this marriage:
1. Wende Nicole (Born) May 1, 1976
2. David Alexander Weddle (Alex) (Born) February 16, 1983

Lucille and Eck's sixth child was Lucille Jane Weddle (Born) February 23, 1947
Married Gary Eugene Gregg in May, 1963
Three children were born to this marriage:
1. Teresa Lynn Gregg Green (Born) May 9, 1964. Married Mark Green. They have twin girls Madison Brooke Green and Tiffany Grace Green b. April 28, 1999
2. Timothy Eugene Gregg (Born) February 3, 1969. Married Angela Bolick Gregg
Tim is divorced but has one daughter Holly Renee Gregg b. Dec. 10, 1989.
His second wife is Lisa Allen Gregg and their children are Trevor Ethan Gregg, b. June 3 2005, and Tessa Everly Gregg, b. Sept. 23, 2010. Tim's step children are Anthony Allen b. June 20, 1997 and Autumn Allen b. Sept. 22, 1998
3. Melissa Carol Gregg Silver (Born) August 6, 1974
Married Daniel Silver and they had two daughter, Sarah Elizabeth b. October 16, 1995, and Emily Rebecca Silver b. June 15, 1997. Melissa divorced and later married Shane Layel, and they have one son Ryan Shane Layel, b. June 17, 2010. Melissa has one step-daughter Chelsea Nicole Layel, b. June 24, 1995

b. *Elise Catherine Helms Creech* (Born April 19, 1913) (Died September 12, 1994)
Married Ernest Clinton Creech November 18, 1938 (Born March 4, 1901)
(Died November 17, 1988)
One child was born to this marriage, a boy
Elise's son: Ernest Clinton Creech, Jr., (Born) September 4, 1950
Married Susan Elaine Conder May 15, 1971 (Born) November 5, 1949
Ernest Jr. and Elaine have two children: a son and a daughter
Chad Reynolds Creech (Born) January 10, 1975
Married Kimberly Lee Williams August 27, 2005 (Born) April 19, 1976
Chad and Kimberly have a son, Cameron Reynolds Creech (Born) April 1, 2009
Keri Elise Creech (Born) July 2, 1977
Married Richard Allen Miller October 19, 2002 (Born) April 22, 1975
Keri and Richard have a daughter, Carson Elise Miller (Born) August 23, 2006, and a son, Aidan James Miller (Born) January 28, 2009
c. *Robert Ralston Helms* (Born August 21, 1915) (Died August 12, 1986)

Ollie Mae Strawn Helms (Born April 5, 1920) (Died September 1, 1990)
Married December 10, 1939. One child was born to this marriage, a girl, Linda

d. *Mary Margaret Helms Rogers* (Born August 18, 1918) (Died December 31, 1975)
Claude Guion Rogers (Born October 27, 1916) (Died February 17, 1966)
Married August 24, 1940
Two children were born to this marriage, 1 boy and 1 girl: Larry Guion Rogers and Lynn
(Dates listed in another section)

e. *Eugene Clayton "Gene" Helms* (Born May 28, 1921) (Died January 15, 1972)
Married Mary Doris McCain (Born August 8, 1924) (Died) July 16, 2009
Two children were born to this marriage:
1. Billy Eugene Helms (Born August 24, 1941) (Died October 12, 2011)
Married Peggy Jean Perry (Born December 11, 1942): two children
were born to this marriage
Child #1: Laurie Ann Helms (Born September 30, 1962): One child Taylor Hollrand
Child #2 David Michael Helms (Born August 16, 1965). Married Jodie Miller: David and
Jodie had two children: Emily Helms and Maggie Helms
2. Mary Kathryn Helms Stubbs (Born July 5, 1944)
Married Murrell Rehm Stubbs, Jr. (Born September 24, 1942)
Two children were born to Mary Kathryn and Murrell:
1. Cynthia Annette Stubbs Carlone (Born September 10, 1962)
Married Vincent Carlone: two children were born to this marriage:
Stratton Ellis-Banks Stubbs Carlone (Born April 5, 1996) (Died) August 16, 2004
Vincent-Murrell McCain Carlone (Born May 3, 1999)
2. Paige Allison Stubbs Norwood (Born December 24, 1965)
Married Matthew Norwood: two children were born to this marriage
James Peyton Boles (Born September 6, 1998)
Emma Kate Norwood (Born July 28, 2002)

f. *Thomas Lee Helms* (Born September 6, 1926) (Died February 11, 1991)
Atha Jeanette (Jean) Bingham Helms (Born May 10, 1931) (Died December 30, 2011)
Married February 19, 1950
Three children were born to this marriage, 1 boy and 2 girls
April 2015, Diane Helms Countryman sent me more dates:
Her mother's full name is: Atha Jeanette Bingham Helms
1. Their oldest child, Phyllis Diane Helms (Countryman) (Born) 1951
Married Michael Naff Hensley in 1972 Divorced in 1980
One son was born to this marriage, Grant Phillip Hensley

Grant Phillip married Amy Moore

One daughter was brought to this marriage, Katie L. Hensley

One son was brought to this marriage, Matthew A. Moore

One son was born to this marriage, Luke Alexander Hensley

2. Second child, Debra Jean Helms (Sineath) (Born) 1955

Married 1973 Allen Medwick McCoy, Jr. Divorced in 1990

Two sons and one daughter were born to this marriage:

1. Eric Quentin McCoy who married Linda Sarver, and two sons were born to his marriage:

Jax B. McCoy and Jet B. McCoy

2. Matthew Clinton McCoy (Died October 26, 2000)

3. Kayla Jean McCoy, married John Paul Sineath, Sr. in 2002

One son was brought to this marriage, John Paul Sineath, Jr.

Kayla Jean McCoy married Larry Dean Plyler, Jr.

One daughter was brought to this marriage, Kinzey J. McManus

One son was born to this marriage, Matthew Ashton Plyler

John Paul Sineath, Jr. married Jamie Ross and one daughter was born to this marriage, Ava G. Sineath

3. Their son Thomas Lee Helms, Jr., (Born 1959) married Lisa Kay Bauer 1988: They had two sons: Thomas Nathan Helms and Cody Maxwell Helms

g. *Charles Bennett "Benny" Helms* (Born July 13, 1934) (Died) September 11, 2011

Married Libby Morris Helms (first wife) One son, Timothy was born to this marriage

Married Judy Collins Helms (Born January 5, 1940): second wife: no children were born to this marriage: Judy had a daughter, Karen, by a previous marriage.

4. **Myrtle Walkup McCain McCain** (Born October 17, 1897) (Died June 7, 1982)

James Kirk McCain (Born September 13, 1892) (Died December 1, 1961)

Married December 6, 1916

Four children were born to this marriage, 1 girl and 3 boys:

a. Mildred Kirk McCain Hinson (Born March 1, 1919) (Died October 23, 2009)

Ross Cecil Hinson (Born December 2, 1911) (Died November 20, 2010).

Married April 2, 1943

four children were born to this marriage; 2 survived, 1 boy and 1 girl

    1. James Richard Hinson b. Jan. 1, 1945. Married Anne Morris June 27, 1971. Anne was born Jan. 17, 1947.

    2. Ronald Kirk Hinson b. Dec. 31, 1950- d. Jan. 2, 1951

    3. Twins Jeannie Eugenia Kay (Jeannie) Hinson and Rachel Ann Hinson b. Nov. 19, 1954 Only Jeannie survived.

b. Robert Dale McCain (Born April 1, 1923) (Died June 10, 2006)

Margaret Robertson Glenn McCain "Margie" (Born February 22, 1929)
(Died February 25, 1996). Married February 23, 1948
Four children were born to this marriage, 3 boys and 1 girl
1. Glenn Dale McCain (Born March 12, 1949)
   Married Marcie Lucille Couick January 28, 1968
   Son of Glenn and Marcie: Mark Glenn McCain (Born June 22, 1970), not married
2. Douglas Kirk McCain (Born January 20, 1956)
   First marriage : Denise Jordan (Born May 27, 1960)
   Second marriage: Janice Gregory (Born July 10, 1957)
3. Rosemary Ann McCain (Born February 27, 1961), not married
4. Michael Paul McCain (Born April 27, 1968), not married

c. Harry Lake McCain (Born July 11, 1926) (Died December 24, 2014)
First Wife: Married Feb. 28, 1952, Betty Jean Lane McCain (b. April 9, 1933-d, July 8, 2011)
Second Wife: Mildred "Millie" Averitt McCain. Married Nov. 24, 2011
The two children of Lake and Betty are as follows:
1. Roger Lake McCain (Born March 1, 1953)
   Married Judy Addis McCain, July 28, 1992. She was born April 7, 1952.
   Roger's oldest son is Shawn Lewis McCain B. July 9, 1976. Married Carrie
   Allyson Huff McCain June 14, 2003. She was born Oct. 6, 1982. Shawn and Carrie
   have three children: Alexander Logan McCain b. April 6, 2004, Ashlyn Blake
   McCain b. Mar. 15, 2006, and Tanner Wyatt McCain b. Dec. 10, 2013
   Roger's second son Joshua Kirk McCain b. May 6, 1979, married Megan Lee
   Gregory McCain April 20, 2013. She was born Oct. 7, 1975.
   Josh and Megan have three children: Brendon Scott Latham b. Aug. 28, 1995,
   Kaden Lake McCain b. Feb. 5, 2003, and daughter Preston Reese McCain
   born Aug. 5, 2005
   Roger's daughter Leah Addis Nail b. Dec. 15, 1978, married John Wayne Nail
   on Nov. 6, 2004. He was born June 26, 1978. They have one son,
   Branden Robert Nail b. June 16, 2010
   Roger's daughter Morgan Rae McCain Chism b. Nov 14, 1978, married
   Thomas Chad Chism on May 17, 2014. He was born Dec. 3, 1980
2. Karen Lane McCain Baxley b. June 29, 1957, married Don William Baxley
   Dec. 5, 1987. He was born April 1, 1959. Karen and Don have two daughters:
   Chandler Lane Baxley b. Mar. 20, 1990, and Bailey Elizabeth Baxley
   b. July 17, 1993. Chandler married Donald Richard Kirkley on April 11, 2015.
   He was born Nov. 20, 1990.

d. Joseph "Joe" Ewart McCain (Born June 19, 1929) (Died October 3, 2013))

Married Betty Wyanne Mullins McCain (Born August 22, 1931) (Living).
Married on November 28, 1954
Two children were born to this marriage, 2 boys

1. John Mullins McCain (Born January 27, 1961)
   Married Rhonda Joy McAteer (August 17, 1985) Rhonda (Born May 26, 1960)
   John and Rhonda have two daughters: Lauren Elizabeth McCain
   (Born January 24, 1989)
   Katelin Ashley McCain (Born January 1, 1994)
2. Joseph Henry McCain (Born July 6, 1963). Married Patricia Khoruy June 3, 1987
   Patricia (Born April 22, 1964)
   Joseph and Patricia have two daughters: Alexandria Mullins McCain
   (Born August 30, 1994)
   Hannah Nichole McCain (Born July 1, 1996)

5. **Robert Maxwell McCain, Sr**. (Born May 31, 1900) (Died December 22, 1984)
Isa Gladys Winslow McCain (Born August 28, 1903) (Died February 9, 1993)
Married November 23, 1932. Three children were born to this marriage, 2 girls and 1 boy
Their children are as follows:
a. *Gladys Elizabeth McCain Kerr* (Born July 22, 1934) (Living). Married on July 28, 1961,
James Donald Kerr (Born January 19, 1934) (Living).
One child was born to this marriage, a boy: James Maxwell Kerr (Born December 1, 1966).
James married Dana Michelle Atchley on May 20, 1995: Dana born Sept. 10, 1967. They
have one son, Williams McCain Kerr (Born March 21, 1997)
b. *Robert Maxwell McCain, Jr.* (Born January 7, 1937) (Living)
Sarah Drake Dodd McCain (Born February 22, 1942) (Living)
Married December 27, 1962
Four children were born to this marriage, all boys : Robert Maxwell McCain, III (born Feb.
27, 1964), David Gibson McCain (born July 4, 1966), Bryan Middleton McCain (born April 6
1969), and Trent Winslow McCain (born Feb. 28, 1971)
c. *Lelia Carole McCain Lewis* (Born December 6, 1940) (Died January 19, 2011)
Married Lee Craig Lewis, Jr. (Born December 7, 1935) (Died December 5, 2008)
Married June 7, 1964
One child was born to this marriage, Andrew Craig Lewis (Born December 6, 1964)

6. **Connie Lee McCain** (Born July 1, 1903) (Died March 14, 1990)
Sadie Roxanna Carter McCain (Born June 21, 1908) (Died August 13, 1962)
Married February 22, 1927. Three children were born to this marriage, 2 girls and 1 boy
Their children are as follows:
a. *Mary Elizabeth McCain Starnes* (Born November 24, 1927) (Now deceased).
Married December 9, 1944

Three children were born to this marriage, 2 girls and 1 boy:

a) Nancy Lucille Starnes (Born June 12, 1946). Married Danny Killian October 4, 1971. Danny born June 10, 1946. Nancy and Danny have two children: Stephanie Killian (Born February 18, 1973) and Travis Killian (Born July 14, 1975)

b) Thomas Samuel Starnes (Born September 27, 1947). Married Jane B. Winchester Feb. 17, 1967. Jane born Oct. 15, 1947. Jane and Tommy have two children: Beth Ann Starnes (Born May 25, 1970). Married Rusty Cook
February 21, 2004 (Born November 4, 1964) and Thomas Lee Starnes
(Born February 19, 1973)
Married Staci Winchester November 29, 2003 (Born June 1, 1969)

c) Barbara Jean (Cookie) Starnes (Born May 1, 1959). Married Dennis Bowers June 20, 1980: divorced: Married Gary Medlin on August 16, 2003 (Born December 31, 1954).
There is a Gary Medlin, Jr. (Born February 22, 1986)

b. *Flora Yvonne McCain Gordon* (Born July 22, 1931) (Died September 21, 1962)
Joe Ware Gordon (Born August 24, 1927) (Died April 25, 1970)
Married October 1952
Three children were born to this marriage, 2 girls and 1 boy: Debbie, Sherry, and Mitchell

a) Debra Jean Gordon (Born October 4, 1953)
Married Dennis Oren Robinson August 21, 1976
Debbie and Dennis have two children: Erica Dawn Robinson (Born July 26, 1981) and Allen Neil Robinson (Born September 20, 1985)

b) Sharon Delores Gordon (Born February 3, 1955). Married Richard Bennett Simpson April 2, 1977 (Born October 9, 1954) Sherry and Rick have three children: Jonathan Bennett Simpson (Born October 20, 1983) and Twins: Lindsey Renae and Michael Joseph Simpson (Born October 18, 1989)

c) Mitchell Joe Gordon (Born September 21, 1962). Married Pamela Glennie Norwood May 21, 1983: Pam born Sept. 2, 1964. Pam and Mitchell had two sons: Adam Matthew Gordon (Born April 8, 1988) and Joseph Mitchell Gordon (Born June 28, 1993)

c. *Robert Lee McCain (*Born December 1, 1933) (Living)
Jo Nell Starnes McCain (Born May 23, 1934) (Living). Married June 9, 1957
Three children were born to this marriage, 2 boys and 1 girl.

a) Michael Robert McCain (Born April 9, 1961) (Died September 28, 1982)

b) Beverly Anne McCain (Born March 21, 1952)
Married Dean Edmund Haney August 18, 1984
Beverly and Dean have two daughters: Lauren Elizabeth Haney Castle (Born May 30, 1988)
Married Levi Castle April 12, 2014 (Born May 19, 1984) and Meredith Brooke Haney (Born January 31, 1993)

c) David Lee McCain (Born April 17, 1986). Married Pamela Rose Winders September 24,

1989, (Born December 13, 1966) David and Pam have one daughter: Sarah Katherine McCain Shaw (Born October 9, 1992) Married Charles Shaw April 26, 2014 (Born August 25, 1987)

7. **Knox Ratchford McCain** (Born May 29, 1907) (Died August 21, 1979)
Ruth Mae Starnes McCain (Born December 27, 1913- Died March 3, 1998)
Married February 25, 1933
Three children were born to this marriage, 2 boys and 1 girl:
Their children are as follows:
a. _William Thomas McCain_ (Born January 1, 1934) (Died December 3, 2010)
First Wife: Annette O'Brian McCain (Born March 17, 1940) (Living)
Married November 21, 1959
Three children were born to this marriage, 3 boys:
a) William Thomas McCain, Jr. (Born January 4, 1960) Not married
b) James Edward McCain (Born November 1, 1961). Married Sharon Elizabeth Meadows on April 12, 1987 (Born January 3, 1965)
Their children are Ashley Nicole (Nikki) McCain (Born April. 25, 1987)
Brittany Morgan McCain Lindsey (Born October 3, 1989). Married Corey Lindsey
Brittany and Corey have a daughter Madeline (Born June 2012)
They are expecting a new arrival.
Timothy Scott McCain: Divorced: Two children: Matthew McCain
(Born February 18, 1988) and Jessica McCain (Born January 26, 1991)
Bill's Second wife: Marlene Starnes Braswell McCain (Born February 9, 1937) (Living)
Married May 6, 1972
b. _Robert Arnold McCain_ (Born March 24, 1935) (Died June 3, 1980)
First wife: Married September 12, 1958, Patricia Anne Guy McCain (Born July 22, 1940) (Died November 11, 2014)
Two children were born to this marriage, 2 girls:
a) Kathy McCain Mandeville: married M. D. Mandeville
b) Lisa Lynn McCain Lowe (Born May 8, 1963)
Married David Luther Lowe February 14, 1983:
(Born June 5, 1963): Lisa and David have three children:
1. Kelly LeAnne Lowe Heatherly (Born August 7, 1984). Married David Matthew Heatherly March 30, 2011 (Born June 17, 1987): Kelly and David have a son: Dakota Lee Heatherly (Born March 15, 2011)
2. Ashley Nicole Lowe (Born March 12, 1987): children: Mya Nicole Lowe (Born December 10, 2007) and Isiah James Bush (Born December 21, 2010)
3. Brandan David Lowe (Born February 25, 1991)
Arnold's Second wife: Alice Louise Street McCain (Born December 7, 1942) (Died October 8, 1997)
Two children were born to this marriage, 1 girl and 1 boy:

Sharron Denise McCain (Born January 4, 1970) Divorced: Has adopted sons.

Brian Alan McCain (Born December 2, 1974). Married Ashley Smiley September 7, 1996, (Born December 5, 1974)

Brian and Ashley have two children: Karleigh Gebrielle Amille McCain (Born July 16, 1997) and Jesse Brian Robert McCain (Born November 29, 2000)

c. *Emma Lynn McCain Twitty (*Born May 29, 1946) (Living)

Boyet A. Twitty, Jr. (Born July 29, 1942) (Living). Married November 24, 1968

Two children were born to this marriage, 1 girl and 1 boy: Allison and Todd:

a) Allison Dione Twitty Batson (Born December 10, 1970), Married Richard Mark Batson on June 26, 1993 (Born May 2, 1971)

Allison and Mark's children: Bristol Knox Batson (Born January 4, 1998), Brody Mark Batson (Born April 4, 2000), and Braylen Jack Batson (Born November 1, 2002)

b) Jonathan Todd Twitty (Born June 5, 1973). Married Debra Parker Twitty December 4, 1999 (Born September 7, 1963).

Debra's son by a previous marriage: D. J. Rushing (Born February 1, 1989). Married Kristen on May 26, 2012 (Born May 9, 1986)

Debra's daughter by a previous marriage: Devane Rushing (Born July 22, 1985)

More information about the Family of Alphonzo Berge and Mary Elizabeth McCain Norwood

Repeating: **Alphonzo Berge Norwood** (Born January 8, 1884) (Died November 10, 1949)

Uncle Berge's wife was my Aunt Mary. Mary Elizabeth McCain Norwood (Born August 30, 1885) (Died June 10, 1972). Children were as follows:

1. *Robert "Rob" Wilson Norwood (*Born September 24, 1908) (Died April 11, 1984)

Rob's wife: Nellie Simpson Norwood (Born September 1, 1915 or 1916) (Died October 26, 1940)

One son: Wilson Walker Norwood (Born May 31, 1941) (Living)

Walker's wife: Patsy Jane Harrell (Born May 31, 1948) (Living). Married July 31, 1971

Walker and Pasty have one child: Patty Lydia Norwood (Born September 7, 1979)

Patty has five children:

2. *Ellen Belk Norwood *(Born September 2, 1911) (Died March 28, 2004)

Ellen's husband: Paul Hueston Baker (Born May 7, 1905) (Died December 17, 1982)

Two children: Mary Dannie Baker (Born July 2, 1936)

Dannie's husband: Harold Jake Vaughn (Born January 25, 1932). Married June 2, 1956

Dannie and Harold have four children: Della, Cathy, Jay, and Amy

Ellen Elizabeth Baker (Born October 4, 1954)

Ellen Elizabeth's husband: Howard Pearson West (Born April 26, 1946), Married October 15, 1986

Ellen Elizabeth and Howard have two children: Matthew Howard West (Born May 7, 1989) and Baker Andrew West (Born December 16, 1991)

3. *Cooper Elizabeth Norwood Starnes *(Born August 21, 1914) (Died April 3, 2008)

Cooper's husband: Brascus Harrison (Jack) Starnes (Born October 16, 1911)
(Died September 19, 1976) Married October 16, 1932 on Jack's birthday
Cooper and Jack had three children:

a) Albert Joseph Starnes (Born September 12, 1939)
Albert's wife: Hazel Cook Starnes (Born July 8, 1932). Married August 27, 1966
Albert and Hazel have three children: Cindy, Debbie, and Danny (Bo)
Bo Starnes (Born December 5, 1968) married Pattie Starnes (Born July 14, 1970)

b) Phonzo Harrison Starnes (Born December 5, 1942)
Phonzo's wife: Clara Hallman (Born September 27, 1945). Married August 18, 1968
Phonzo and Clara have two children: Joseph Chad Starnes (Born October 26, 1975) and Seth Harrison Starnes (Born November 20, 1977)

c) Cora Elizabeth (Libby) Starnes (Born September 20, 1947)
Libby's husband: Charles Eddie Kiser (Born June 8, 1938). Married October 27, 1967
Libby and Eddie have two children: Leslie Annetti Kiser (Born April 1970) and Glenn David Kiser (Born September 30, 1973). Grandchild Zoe Alexis Kiser (Born December 18, 1997)

4. *Myrtle Norwood Simpson* (Born June 20, 1917) (Died March 13, 2003)
Myrtle's husband: Simmie Hazel Simpson, Sr. (Born April 14, 1914) (Died January 15, 1981)
Married October 8, 1939
Myrtle and Simmie had two children:
Phyllis Simpson Garner and Simmie Hazel Simpson
a) Phyllis Simpson Garner married Gerald Garner. They have three children: **Ashley Garner** who married Nathan Blackon (Their children are twins Carter and Caroline and a daughter Charlotte), **Holly Simpson Garner** whose husband is Jason and their son is Zach, and **Benjamin Garner.**
b) Hazel Simpson married Sarah Simpson and they had four children:
Neely Erin Crawford, born May 11, 1979,
Brian Heath Simpson, born May 20, 1981,
Kelly Laine Simpson, born March 10, 1990, and
Travis Grant Simpson, born May 20, 1981. (Died May 22, 1981)
Hazel and Sarah's grandchildren: Branden Hugh Crawford, born September 7, 2005
and Sarah Ann Crawford, born October 11, 2006

5. *William Franklin (Bill) Norwood* (Born May 25, 1920) (Died September 25, 1990)
Bill's wife: Ruth McManus Norwood, living

6. *Samuel Blanton (Pete) Norwood* (Born November 9, 1922) (Died April 9, 1963)
Pete's wife: Maude Stewart (Born November 20, 1922) (Died January 24, 2000)

7. *Jack Newton Norwood* (Born September 18, 1926) (Died October 28, 2007)
Jack's wife: Maxine Norwood (Died March 3, 2008)
Daughter: Marcella Norwood Saunders: Husband Chip Saunders
Marcella and Chip had a son, Jeff, who had two sons: Jake and Bradley